PATCHWORK PLUS

EASY ONE-BLOCK QUILTS WITH SEASONAL APPLIQUÉ

GERALYN J. POWERS

Martingale®
Create with Confidence

Patchwork Plus:
Easy One-Block Quilts with Seasonal Appliqué
© 2013 by Geralyn J. Powers

Martingale®
19021 120th Ave. NE, Ste. 102
Bothell, WA 98011-9511 USA
ShopMartingale.com

Printed in China
18 17 16 15 14 13   8 7 6 5 4 3 2 1

Library of Congress Cataloging-in-Publication Data is available upon request.

ISBN: 978-1-60468-261-8

Mission Statement

Dedicated to providing quality products and service to inspire creativity.

CREDITS
President and CEO: Tom Wierzbicki
Editor in Chief: Mary V. Green
Design Director: Paula Schlosser
Managing Editor: Karen Costello Soltys
Acquisitions Editor: Karen M. Burns
Technical Editor: Ursula Reikes
Copy Editor: Tiffany Mottet
Production Manager: Regina Girard
Cover and Interior Designer: Adrienne Smitke
Photographer: Brent Kane
Illustrator: Ann Marra

DEDICATION
To Keith, for your constant encouragement, assurance, and selfless support.

CONTENTS

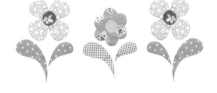

Introduction

A very wise man I know said that being creative will "help you enjoy life. . . . It gives a renewal, a spark of enthusiasm, and a zest for life." In my experience, that is very true. Quite obviously, quilting is my chosen venue for creativity, and probably yours as well, since you're reading this. There's something wonderful about choosing fabric and a design and taking the time to stitch a beautiful quilt. It certainly adds a spark of joy to the mundane tasks of life, not to mention all the fun of "requiring" a visit to the quilt shop!

My favorite quilts are pieced, usually with many different fabrics, and they have a bit of appliqué. I like the appliqué because it lends itself to personal creativity. I have learned to enjoy each step in the process; playing with color, picking a block that works well with appliqué, and often making the quilt for a cherished someone or a special occasion, simply put, brings joy.

I also appreciate learning about the history of quilting, about those women of long ago who shared small pieces of fabric to brighten each other's lives, and then passed on the lessons of their creativity. Both my grandmothers and a great grandmother were beautiful quilters and seamstresses. I watched and learned from them as I grew up, continually marveling that their need for function was sparked by their desire to be creative in the process. Their bed quilts were not just necessary, they were also beautiful—a great lesson for life! We may be required to do something, but the choice to do it well, or in a uniquely individual way, is that spark of creativity that adds purpose to life.

This book is full of quilts made for fun, joy, nostalgia, and the enjoyment of the creative process. Hopefully they will bring smiles and happy thoughts. Enjoy making them and giving them away. And most of all, enjoy the journey.

Fabric Selection

Choose only 100% cotton, quilt-shop-quality fabric. This refers to manufacturers that sell primarily to quilt shops. When you put a lot of time and work into a quilt, you want it to last for many years and washings. There is a big difference in the quality of fabric; the old adage "you get what you pay for" is very applicable. Quilt shops buy from those manufacturers who use the best goods, dyes, and finishes. Cotton that has been properly dyed, woven, and finished has great "memory" and is very durable and delightful to work with. Good-quality fabric is easily sewn, pressed with or without steam, washed, and folded. If properly cared for, it maintains its color and will wear well for a very long time.

About half of all quilters believe in prewashing fabric and the other half do not. I personally do not prewash fabrics before piecing, because I like the little extra crispness given by the finish. With that said, if I am concerned about a particular fabric bleeding, especially a batik, prewashing is very sensible. I do like to wash quilts after they are quilted and bound. A quilt that has been gently washed and dried has a soft, aged look that begs the owner to cuddle up with it. Often I wash a quilt before I give it away because it looks so lovely.

Wash quilts in cold water with a very mild detergent and use a color catcher in the wash to absorb any extra or bleeding dyes. Color catchers are available in the laundry section of your grocery store. They look like dryer sheets and are simply thrown in the washing machine with the quilt. I then dry my quilts in the dryer on a low-heat setting.

Choosing colors can be a challenge for many quilters. One simple way to effectively combine colors is to pick a "focus" or main fabric. The focus could also be a photo, a piece of pottery, or other artwork instead of fabric. Select fabrics that match the colors in the focus piece, placing them next to each other for effect. Perhaps you'll want to go a shade darker in one fabric and a shade lighter in another. Often, when I need to choose a color combination, I will pull out everything I have in my stash that might go with a focus piece. By placing the fabrics on a bed, the floor, or a design wall and standing back for a good look, you will learn to see what works and what doesn't. Of course, a new project always requires a trip to the quilt shop to see if there's anything that needs to be added! Today, most fabric companies produce fabric lines featuring several color combinations that go well together, making the selection process easier.

For this book, I made several quilts using a tone-on-tone color palette, which means choosing a half dozen or more fabrics of one color, with

Three colors in a variety of textures and shades.

varying textures and shades. Perhaps a quilt calls for several grays, so choosing various patterns, such as a polka dot, plaid, mottled, dark-on-medium gray print, and so forth, will make a beautiful and interesting quilt. Texture, or the way the colors give movement or interest to the fabric surface, can add a lovely dimension to a quilt. You know a fabric has interesting texture when you want to touch it!

A scrappy quilt can be made by using many different fabrics. My favorite kind of quilt is what I call "controlled scrappy." Choosing only certain colors, prints, and textures, such as all reds and pinks or all grays and blues, creates a controlled scrappy look. It is also important to pay attention to the scale of prints. Large prints work best in large pieces. Small prints are much more effective in a quilt with a lot of small pieces, maintaining a traditional scrappy look.

I highly recommend using a design wall when assembling your quilt. It is so helpful to place blocks in the preferred order and then stand across the room to look at them. This allows you to see what is well placed and what needs to be moved. Colors can change or be affected by what is placed next to them. Working on a design wall also helps you decide border and even binding colors.

When all is said and done, the fabric is certainly one of, if not the most important element in the quilt. Choosing fabrics can also be one of the most exciting parts of the project. Enjoy it! When you use colors that you love, you will create quilts that you love.

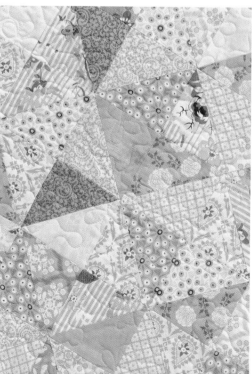
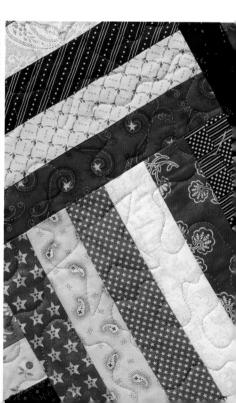

Basic Quiltmaking Techniques

On the following pages, you'll find basic information for making the quilts in this book. If you require more help, visit ShopMartingale.com /HowtoQuilt for free downloadable information.

HALF-SQUARE-TRIANGLE UNITS

Two blocks in this book use half-square-triangle units. Place two squares of the same size with right sides together, and draw a diagonal line on the wrong side of the lighter-colored square. Stitch ¼" from both sides of the line. Cut on the marked line. Press as instructed. You'll get two half-square-triangle units from each pair of squares.

Mark diagonal.

Stitch ¼" from line.

Cut along line.

Press.

FOLDED-TRIANGLE UNITS

Some blocks use the stitch-and-fold method to add a triangle to another square or rectangle. Draw a diagonal line on the wrong side of the smaller square. Place the smaller square on top of the larger unit with right sides together and corners aligned. Stitch on the line and press toward the corner. If the corners do not match up, time to use the seam ripper! Trim the seam allowances to ¼".

PRESSING

Pressing is as important as stitching when it comes to accuracy. Correct pressing will enhance piecing. Practice the habit of pressing every seam before you sew another seam across it. It's very helpful to press the seam on the wrong side to set the threads before pressing the seam allowances in one direction or the other. It is ideal to press toward the darker fabric, so lay the darker part of the unit on top when placing it on the ironing board. Fold the darker piece over and gently press toward the darker side. Arrows are used in the illustrations to indicate which direction to press.

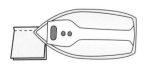

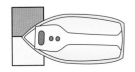

If using steam, be careful not to distort the shapes of the pieced units. Press by simply lowering the iron and raising it again. Don't move the iron in a back-and-forth motion as that tends to distort the pieced unit.

FUSIBLE APPLIQUÉ

If you haven't used appliqué to enhance your quilts, the simplicity of fusible web will delight you and give you so many opportunities to create beautiful quilts. There are several good brands of fusible web on the market. If you don't already have a favorite, purchase small amounts of several brands and try them out. Use only lightweight fusible web. The heavyweight and ultra-hold types are made for iron-on only; stitching around the appliqués will gum up your needle and sewing machine. Read all of the manufacturer's instructions carefully as each brand varies a little in use.

In this book, all patterns are reversed for fusible appliqué and are ready to trace.

Preparing Appliqués

1. Trace the pattern onto the paper side of the fusible web, leaving at least ½" between shapes, and roughly cut them outside the drawn line.

With pieces larger than a couple of inches, it's helpful to remove bulk by cutting away the center of the paper shape ¼" inside the drawn line. This also reduces stiffness when several pieces are layered on top of each other.

2. Iron the shapes to the wrong side of the fabric, being careful not to distort the shape. Carefully cut on the drawn line; your appliqué will be exactly the shape you cut! Peel off the paper and place the units on the fabric, layering back pieces first and working toward the

top layer, following the pattern placement. Press the units in place.

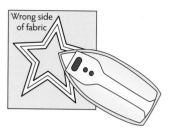

3. Use an open-toe machine appliqué foot for the best results as it allows you to see where you are stitching. Many machines have other great options for making appliqué look professional. For a hand-done effect, the needle-down feature, mirror imaging, half-speed stitching, and double-blanket stitching are all helpful features.

For the look of invisible appliqué, use a fine machine embroidery thread in the same color as the fabric. If you want a folk-art or hand-sewn look, use a heavier topstitching thread in a matching or coordinating color. I like appliquéing all pieces in black or dark brown for a "country" look. The possibilities are endless and, through the process of choosing, you leave your own creative mark.

If your machine's bobbin case has a special eye for use with embroidery stitches, inserting your bobbin thread through this eye will provide additional tension and may help you to achieve perfect stitches. It also allows you to use one color in the bobbin throughout the appliqué and change only the top thread, using different colors as desired. (When the thread goes through the eye of the bobbin case, the tension is consistent, allowing the thread colors to be consistent on the seam front and back.)

Making Fabric Opaque

Now and then a quilt calls for a light fabric appliquéd over a dark background. An example is the white ghost on the black print in "Step into Halloween" on page 25. When you need to make a fabric opaque, press a white lightweight knit, iron-on interfacing to a section of the fabric before cutting out the shape. After the interfacing is ironed on, treat the interfaced fabric like one layer. Press the fusible web to the wrong side of the fabric, which will technically be the right side of the interfacing. Fuse, cut, and stitch around the appliqué as you would any other piece of fabric.

Using a Pressing Sheet

For ease when combining several appliqué pieces into a unit, use a pressing sheet. A pressing sheet is a reusable, double-sided sheet made from ultra-high-temperature material with a non-stick coating. It allows you to press several units together, making it easier to fuse them as one piece to the background of your project. It's also easier to accurately align pieces on a pressing sheet and then transfer them to the quilt, rather than trying to place many pieces on a large quilting surface at once. Pressing sheets are available at your local quilt shop or on the Internet.

DECORATIVE STITCHING

Decorative stitching or embroidery can enhance appliqué designs. I like to use the decorative stitch on my machine that looks like tiny rickrack. If you don't have a stitch exactly like the sample, try a similar stitch. Choose the desired color of thread and stitch stems, rope, spider legs, frosting, and other details for an added dimension.

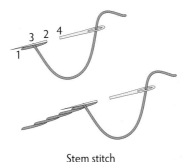

Decorative machine stitch for applique

A machine double stitch—a straight stitch that goes back and forth before making the next stitch—can look like hand embroidery. I use it to define mouths, eyebrows, and lines in pumpkins, for example.

Machine double stitch

If your machine doesn't have this stitch, choose another decorative stitch or hand embroider using a stem stitch.

Stem stitch

FINISHING

You have many choices when it comes to finishing a quilt. Deciding on backing fabric, batting, and stitching designs are all part of the creativity. Each decision contributes to the outcome and charm of the quilt.

For help with any of these things, go to ShopMartingale.com/HowtoQuilt. For assistance with binding see below.

Binding

The quilts in this book include yardage for binding that is cut 2½" wide. I use the traditional double-fold method and always join binding strips with diagonal seams, which are less bulky and therefore less noticeable.

1. Overlap the ends of the binding strips right sides together. Sew diagonally from corner to corner, marking before sewing if desired. Trim off the outside corner and press the seam allowances open. Press the strip in half with wrong sides together.

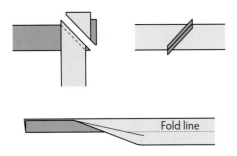

2. Leaving an 8" to 10" tail, start sewing the binding to the quilt top using a ¼"-wide seam allowance. End the stitching ¼" from the corner of the quilt and backstitch. Turn the quilt so that you will be stitching down the next side. Fold the binding up, away from the quilt, and then back down onto itself, parallel with the edge of the quilt top. Begin stitching at the edge, backstitching to secure. Repeat on all corners.

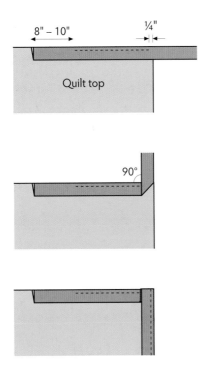

3. Stop sewing when you are about 12" from the starting point. Lay out the beginning tail and overlap the ending tail, the same width as the binding. For example, because the binding is cut 2½" wide, the overlap will be 2½". You can even use the width of your binding as a measurement guide. Sew the two ends together on the diagonal. Trim, leaving a ¼"-wide seam allowance and press. Reposition the binding on the quilt and finish sewing. This is a wonderful finish; no one will be able to tell where you started or ended, and it can be used with any width of binding.

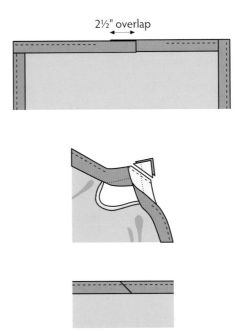

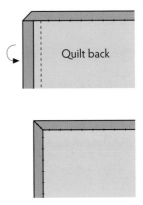

4. Fold the edge of the binding to the back of the quilt and hand stitch in place, covering the stitching line and mitering the corners.

Petals for the Table

With the change of seasons, it's nice to change the quilts you use in home decor. I really enjoy using quilts as tablecloths. However, I haven't yet had the courage to serve dinner on one and probably never will! This quilt was designed for a table and brings spring right into the house. It looks lovely on a round, square, or rectangular table, and provides an additional way to display handiwork.

MATERIALS

Yardage is based on 42"-wide fabric. Fat quarters measure approximately 18" x 21". Fat eighths measure approximately 9" x 21".

1½ yards of red floral for outer border
1¼ yards of pink-on-white floral for appliqué background
¾ yard of small-scale red print for inner square, inner border, and binding
⅝ yard of green tone-on-tone fabric for middle border, stem appliqués, and leaf appliqués
⅝ yard of small-scale red-on-white floral for setting triangles
½ yard of small-scale gray print for blocks and flower appliqués

⅓ yard of small-scale pink print for blocks
Fat quarter of white-on-red mini-dot fabric for flower appliqués
Fat eighth of small-scale pink print for flower-center appliqués
4 yards of fabric for backing
8" x 8" square of pink tone-on-tone fabric for flower-center appliqués
65" x 65" piece of batting
1 yard of lightweight fusible web for appliqués
Thread in coordinating colors for appliqués

CUTTING

All measurements include ¼"-wide seam allowances. Cut all strips across the width of fabric unless otherwise instructed.

The appliqué patterns for pieces A–F are on page 16. For information on preparing and cutting pieces for fusible appliqué, refer to "Fusible Appliqué" on page 8.

From the small-scale gray print, cut:
3 strips, 3" x 42"; crosscut into 32 squares, 3" x 3"

From the small-scale pink print for blocks, cut:
3 strips, 3" x 42"; crosscut into 32 squares, 3" x 3"

From the green tone-on-tone fabric, cut:
1 strip, 3" x 42"; crosscut into 8 squares, 3" x 3"
8 strips, 1¼" x 42"; crosscut into:
    2 strips, 1¼" x 28½"
    2 strips, 1¼" x 30"
    8 strips, 1¼" x 8"
    8 strips 1¼" x 9½"

From the pink-on-white floral, cut:
4 strips, 9½" x 30"
1 strip, 2" x 42"; crosscut into 4 strips, 2" x 8"

Continued on page 13

Designed, pieced, and quilted by Geralyn Powers
FINISHED QUILT: 61" x 61" ▪ FINISHED BLOCK: 7½" x 7½"

From the small-scale red print, cut:
2 strips, 2" x 42"; crosscut into:
  2 strips, 2" x 17"
  2 strips, 2" x 20"
1 square, 2" x 2"
7 strips, 2½" x 42"

From the small-scale red-on-white floral, cut:
2 squares, 17" x 17"; cut the squares in half diagonally to make 4 triangles. The triangles are
  oversized and will be trimmed later.

From the red floral, cut:
7 strips, 7" x 42"

From the white-on-red mini-dot fabric, cut:
8 A

From the remaining small-scale gray print, cut:
4 B

From the small-scale pink print for flower
centers, cut:
8 C

From the pink tone-on-tone fabric, cut:
4 D

From the remaining green tone-on-tone fabric,
cut:
12 E
24 F

MAKING THE BLOCKS

Arrange four gray 3" squares, four pink 3" squares,
and one green 3" square. Sew the squares into
horizontal rows. Press the seam allowances away
from the pink squares. Sew the rows together to
complete a block. Press the seam allowances away
from the center row. The block should measure
8" x 8". Make eight blocks.

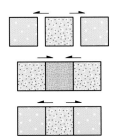

Make 8.

ASSEMBLING THE QUILT CENTER

1. Sew a pink-on-white floral 2" x 8" strip
   between two blocks. Press the seam allowances toward the center strip. Make two units.
   Sew a red 2" square between two pink-on-
   white floral 2" x 8" strips. Press the seam
   allowances away from the red square. Sew the
   two block rows to the center unit. Press the
   seam allowances toward the center unit.

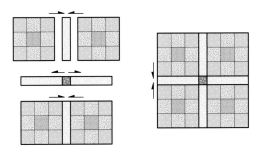

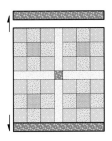

2. Sew the red 2" x 17" strips to the top and
   bottom of the block unit. Press the seam allowances toward the red strips. Sew the red 2" x 20"
   strips to opposite sides of the unit. Press the
   seam allowances toward the red strips.

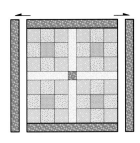

3. Sew two red-on-white floral triangles to opposite sides of the block unit from step 2. Press the seam allowances toward the triangles. Repeat to sew two red-on-white floral triangles to the remaining opposite sides. Trim the oversized triangles ¼" from the points of the center square so you end up with a unit that measures 28½" x 28½".

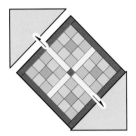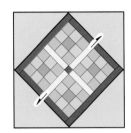

4. Sew the green 1¼" x 28½" strips to the top and bottom of the unit from step 3. Press the seam allowances toward the green strips. Sew the green 1¼" x 30" strips to opposite sides of the quilt. Press the seam allowances toward the green strips.

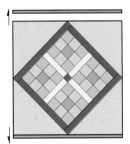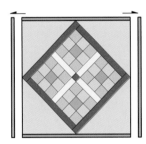

ASSEMBLING THE QUILT TOP

1. Arrange the appliqué pieces on each of the pink-on-white print 9½" x 30" rectangles. Extend the flower stem into the seam allowance to touch the raw edge of the fabric. Fuse and stitch the stems, leaves, flowers, and centers in place. Make four borders.

Make 4.

2. Sew two of the appliquéd borders to opposite sides of the quilt. Press the seam allowances toward center of the quilt.

3. Sew two green 1¼" x 8" strips to the top and bottom of a pieced block. Press the seam allowances toward the green strips. Sew two green 1¼" x 9½" strips to opposite sides of the block. Press the seam allowances toward the green strips. The block should measure 9½" x 9½". Make four blocks.

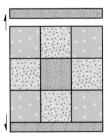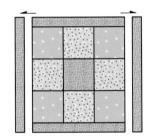

Make 4.

4. Sew two blocks from step 3 to opposite ends of the two remaining appliquéd panels. Press the seam allowances toward the appliquéd panel. Sew the units to the top and bottom of the quilt. Press the seam allowances toward the quilt center. Join the red floral 7" x 42" outer-border strips end to end to make one long strip. Cut two 7" x 42" borders and sew them to opposite sides of the quilt. Press the seam allowances toward the borders. Cut two 7" x 61" borders and sew them to the top and bottom of the quilt. Press the seam allowances toward the borders.

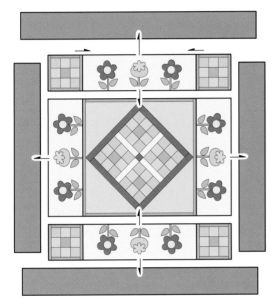

Quilt assembly

FINISHING THE QUILT

Refer to "Finishing" on page 9 as needed.

1. Layer the quilt top, batting, and backing (pieced horizontally); baste. Quilt as desired. I quilted a large floral design on the outside borders and a smaller floral design around the appliqués and on the setting triangles. There are curved lines quilted in the blocks, and stitching around each appliqué piece to anchor it and give it definition.

2. Using the red 2½"-wide strips, sew the binding to the quilt.

Holiday Option

Choose whimsical Christmas fabric and use the alternate appliqué designs provided to create "Visions of Sugarplums" from this same pattern. The colorful tossed candies and treats will beckon friends and family to celebrate the season. Follow the same steps, but instead of using the floral appliqué, stitch the candy, cupcakes, and gingerbread men as shown in the quilt photo. Use the small gingerbread man pattern (B) from "Gingermania" on page 51. The rest of the appliqué patterns (A–I) are on page 17. Refer to "Decorative Stitching" on page 9 to embellish the gingerbread men with frosting. This is a perfect holiday quilt to hang on a wall, toss over a sofa, or use on the table.

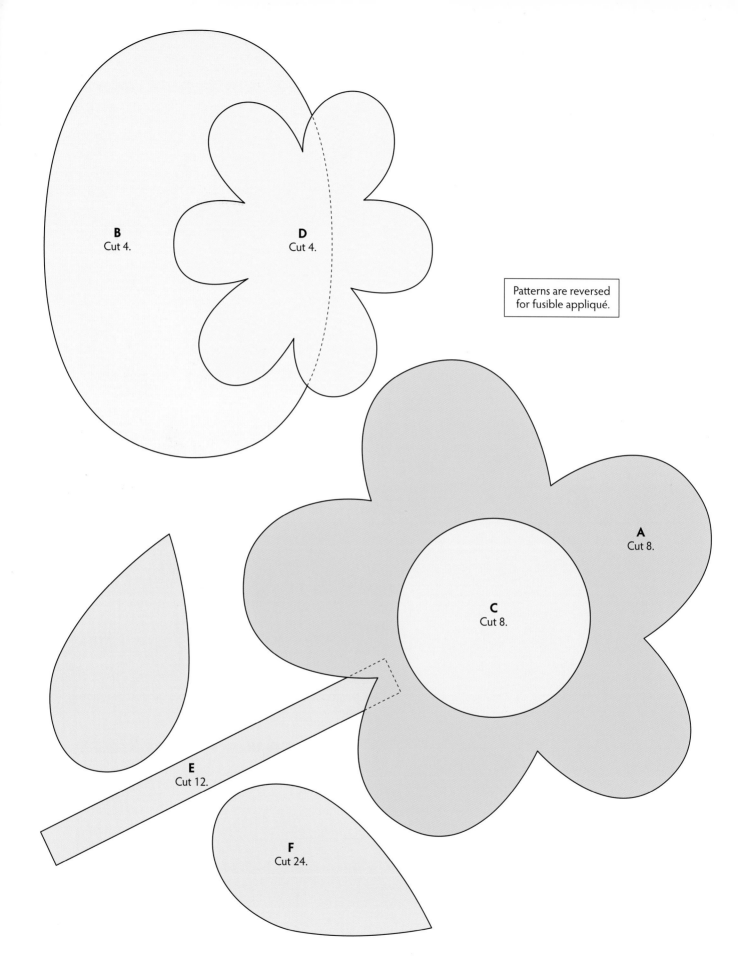

B
Cut 4.

D
Cut 4.

Patterns are reversed
for fusible appliqué.

A
Cut 8.

C
Cut 8.

E
Cut 12.

F
Cut 24.

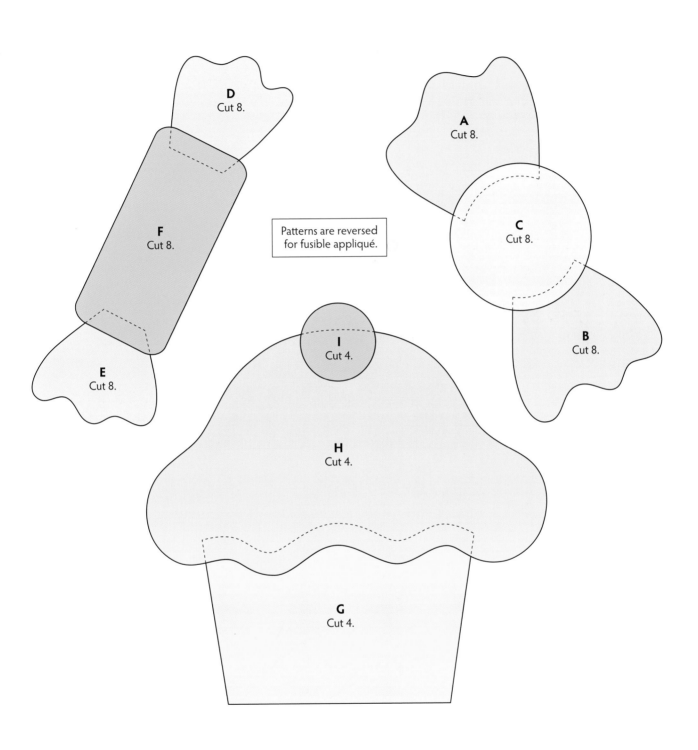

D
Cut 8.

A
Cut 8.

F
Cut 8.

Patterns are reversed
for fusible appliqué.

C
Cut 8.

E
Cut 8.

B
Cut 8.

I
Cut 4.

H
Cut 4.

G
Cut 4.

Designed, pieced, and quilted by Geralyn Powers

FINISHED QUILT: 64½" x 72½" ▪ **FINISHED BLOCK: 8" x 8"**

Bells Are Ringing

Christmas is my favorite holiday, and I love using not only quilts in traditional colors, but quilts that enhance home decor. This design reminds me of a very old Christmas carol, "I Heard the Bells on Christmas Day," and a wish for peace on earth. Because this quilt is not made with traditional holiday colors, it can be left out all year. It would also make a lovely anniversary or wedding gift, using the bride's colors and having guests sign the light squares.

MATERIALS

Yardage is based on 42"-wide fabric.

2¼ yards of gray floral print for outer border and binding

⅓ yard *each* of 6 gray prints for blocks

⅓ yard *each* of 6 pink prints for blocks

1⅞ yards of white-and-gray print for blocks and appliqué background

⅝ yard of red solid for inner border and appliqués

⅓ yard of gray polka-dot fabric for bell appliqués

¼ yard of pink solid for border on appliqué background

¼ yard of gray solid for ironwork appliqué

4½ yards of fabric for backing

70" x 78" piece of batting

1 yard of lightweight fusible web for appliqués

Gray and red thread for appliqués

CUTTING

All measurements include ¼"-wide seam allowances.

Appliqué patterns for pieces A–F are on pages 22 and 23. For information on preparing and cutting pieces for fusible appliqué, refer to "Fusible Appliqué" on page 8.

From the white-and-gray print, cut:
18 strips, 2½" x 42"; crosscut into 288 squares, 2½" x 2½"
1 rectangle, 13½" x 21½"

From *each* of the 6 gray and 6 pink prints for blocks, cut:
2 strips, 4½" x 42"; crosscut into 24 rectangles, 2½" x 4½" (288 total)

From the pink solid, cut:
2 strips, 2" x 42"; crosscut into:
    2 strips, 2" x 16½"
    2 strips, 2" x 21½"

From the red solid, cut:
8 strips, 1½" x 42"
3 A
1 *each* of B, C, and D

From the gray polka-dot fabric, cut:
3 F

From the gray solid, cut:
1 E

From the gray floral print, cut:
8 strips, 7½" x 42"
7 strips, 2½" x 42"

MAKING THE BLOCKS

1. Referring to "Folded-Triangle Units" on page 7, sew the white-and-gray 2½" squares to one end of the gray print and pink print 2½" x 4½" rectangles. Make a total of 288 folded-triangle units. Press the seam allowances *toward* the triangles on 144 pink units, and *away* from the triangles on the other 144 gray units.

Press 144 toward the triangles.

Press 144 away from the triangles.

2. Join the units from step 1 in pairs, noting the direction of the pressed seam allowances. Sew the pairs together to make 72 half-block units. Then sew the half-block units together to complete the block. Press the seam allowances as indicated. The block should measure 8½" x 8½". Make 36 blocks.

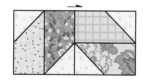

Make 144.   Make 72.

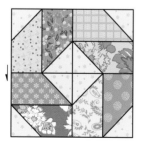

Make 36.

ASSEMBLING THE QUILT TOP

1. Sew two pink 2" x 21½" strips to opposite sides of the white-and-gray 13½" x 21½" rectangle. Sew two pink 2" x 16½" strips to the top and bottom of the rectangle. Press the seam allowances toward the pink strips.

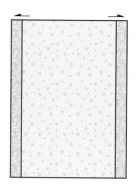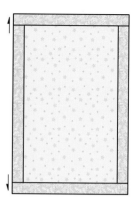

2. Lay out the pieced blocks and the white-and-gray rectangle as shown, with one row of six blocks above the rectangle and three rows of six blocks below it. Rotate the blocks or rearrange them until you are satisfied with the layout. Sew the blocks together to complete each row, pressing the seam allowances in opposite directions from row to row.

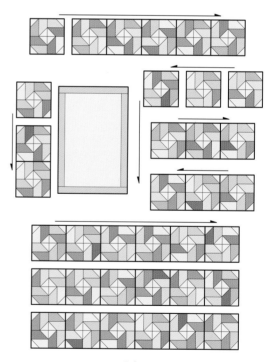

Quilt layout

3. Sew the three short rows of blocks together, pressing all seam allowances in one direction. Join this section to the right of the rectangle.

Sew the three single blocks together and join them to the left of the rectangle. Then sew one row of six blocks to the top of this unit to make the top section of the quilt.

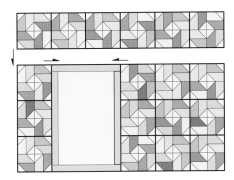

4. Working on the framed rectangle, center the top of the ironwork piece ½" above the pink border; fuse and stitch the piece in place. Arrange the bells, ribbons and bows on the rectangle. Fuse and stitch the appliqués in place.

¾"

5. Join the three remaining block rows to complete the bottom of the quilt. Join the top and bottom sections. Press the seam allowances in one direction.

6. Join the red 1½" x 42" inner-border strips end to end to make one long strip. Cut two

1½" x 56½" strips and sew them to opposite sides of the quilt. Press the seam allowances toward the red strips. Cut two 1½" x 50½" strips and sew them to the top and bottom of the quilt. Press the seam allowances toward the red strips.

7. Join the gray floral 7½" x 42" outer-border strips end to end to make one long strip. Cut two strips 7½" x 58½" and sew them to opposite sides of the quilt. Press the seam allowances toward the gray strips. Cut two 7½" x 64½" strips and sew them to the top and bottom of quilt. Press the seam allowances toward the gray strips.

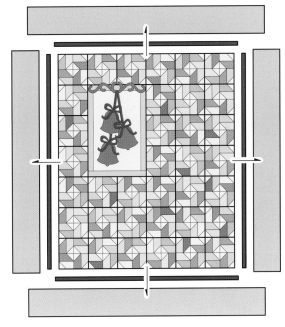

Quilt assembly

FINISHING THE QUILT

Refer to "Finishing" on page 9 as needed.

1. Layer the quilt top, batting, and backing; baste. Quilt as desired. I machine quilted an overall curls-and-feathers design on the blocks, and a small linear echo on the appliqué background.

2. Using the gray floral 2½"-wide strips, sew the binding to the quilt.

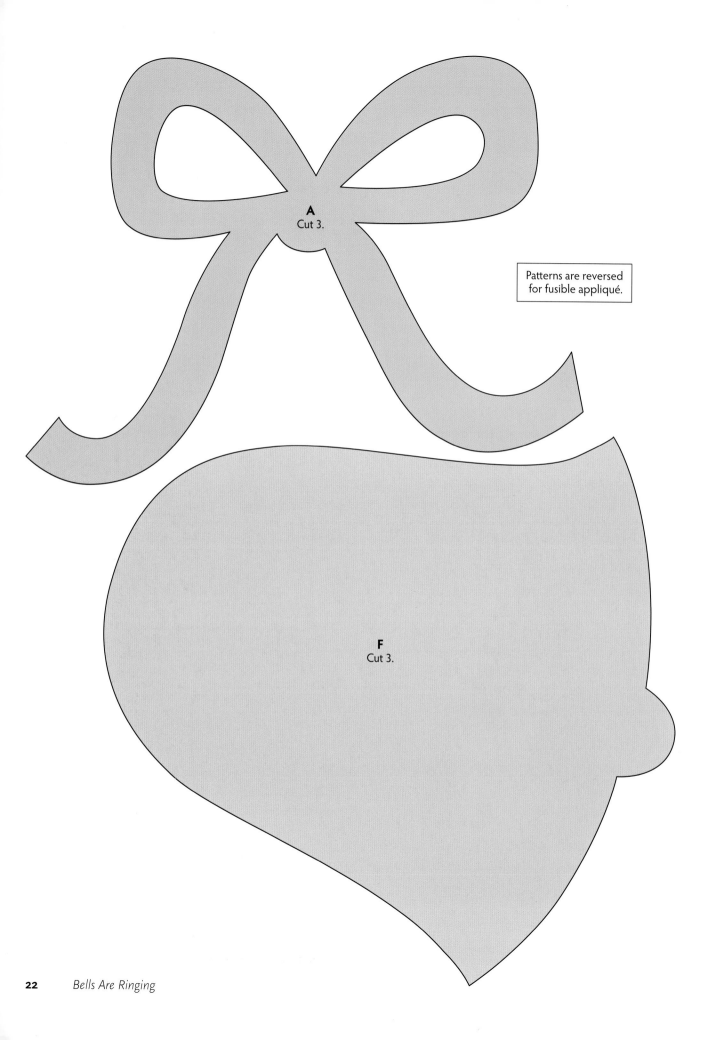

A
Cut 3.

Patterns are reversed
for fusible appliqué.

F
Cut 3.

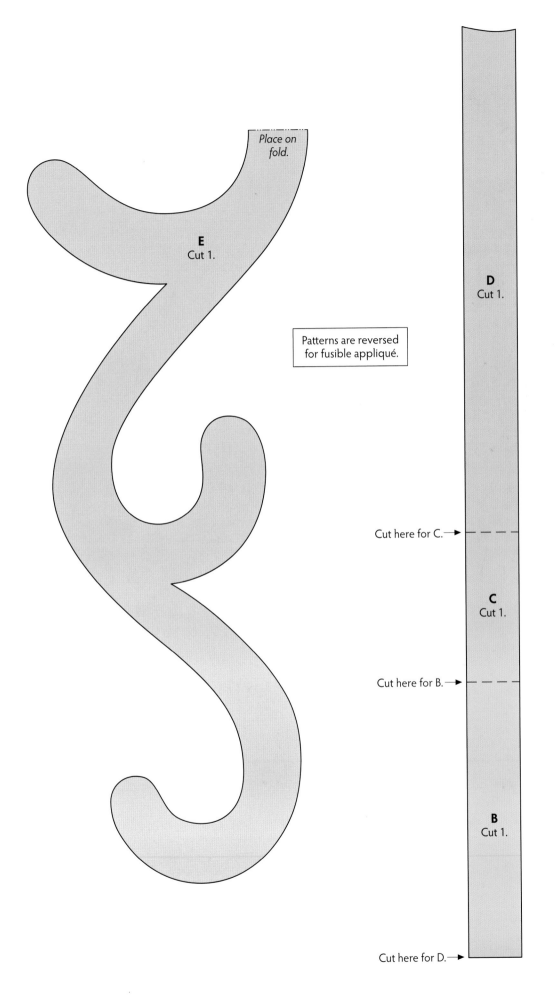

Place on fold.

E
Cut 1.

Patterns are reversed
for fusible appliqué.

D
Cut 1.

Cut here for C. →

C
Cut 1.

Cut here for B. →

B
Cut 1.

Cut here for D. →

Designed, pieced, and quilted by Geralyn Powers
FINISHED QUILT: 56½" x 64½" ■ FINISHED BLOCK: 8" x 8"

Step into Halloween

I never went trick-or-treating as a child. In our small community, there was a highly anticipated and traditional Halloween party at the school. After secretly preparing costumes, families would gather at the school where children would parade by age and grade, showing off their disguises. Judges awarded silver dollars for prizes, a grand thing in those days. Bags of candy were given to all and the costumes were talked about for days after. It was so exciting; I never felt I had missed anything.

MATERIALS

Yardage is based on 42"-wide fabric. Fat quarters measure approximately 18" x 21".

1¼ yards *total* of gray tone-on-tone fabric for Checkerboard blocks

⅓ yard *each* of 2 black tone-on-tone fabrics for Checkerboard blocks and bat, pumpkin, skull, ghost, and Frankenstein appliqués

½ yard of white-on-white print for ghost and skull appliqués

10 fat quarters of assorted gray tone-on-tone fabric for blocks

2 fat quarters of orange tone-on-tone fabric for pumpkins

2 fat quarters of lime-green print for letters, spider, and Frankenstein's head appliqués

Fat quarter of yellow print for moon and star appliqués

Fat quarter of black print for witch's hat appliqué

10" x 10" square of orange-and-black striped fabric for witch's shoes appliqué

10" x 10" square of multicolored-striped fabric for witch's hat band appliqué

10" x 10" square of purple print for Frankenstein's hair appliqué

5" x 12" scrap of striped fabric for Frankenstein's shirt appliqué

3" x 6" scrap of orange-and-black dot fabric for Frankenstein's bow tie

5" x 5" scrap of orange-dot fabric for letters "o" and "r"

2" x 5" scrap of brown solid for pumpkin stem appliqués

⅝ yard of multicolored-striped fabric for binding

4 yards of fabric for backing

60" x 68" piece of batting

1 yard of white lightweight knit, iron-on interfacing for appliqués

3 yards of lightweight fusible web for appliqués

Two black buttons, ½" diameter, for spider eyes

Black thread for appliqués and decorative stitching

CUTTING

All measurements include ¼"-wide seam allowances. Cut all strips across the width of the fabric unless otherwise indicated.

The appliqué patterns for pieces A–DD are on pages 29–39. For information on preparing and cutting pieces for fusible appliqué, refer to "Fusible Appliqué" on page 8, and "Making Fabric Opaque" on page 9.

From the gray tone-on-tone fabric for Checkerboard blocks, cut:

4 strips, 4½" x 42"; crosscut into 36 squares, 4½" x 4½"

5 strips, 2½" x 42"; crosscut into 72 squares, 2½" x 2½"

6 strips, 1½" x 42"

Continued on page 26

From *1* of the black tone-on-tone fabrics, cut:
6 strips, 1½" x 42"

From *each* of the 10 assorted gray tone-on-tone fat quarters, cut:
4 squares, 8½" x 8½" (40 total; 2 are extra)

From the orange tone-on-tone fabrics, cut:
1 A
1 D

From the *second* black tone-on-tone fabric, cut:
3 N
2 H
2 I
2 each of P, T, C, F, and Y
1 each of B, G, Z, and AA

From the brown solid, cut:
2 E

From the orange-and-black striped fabric, cut:
1 J and 1 reversed

From the black print, cut:
1 each of K and M

From the multicolored striped fabric, cut:
1 L

From the lime-green prints, cut:
Letters for words "trick" and "treat"
1 R
1 W

From *each* of the white-on-white print *and* interfacing, cut:
1 X
4 BB
I O
2 Q

From the striped fabric, cut:
1 U

From the purple print, cut:
1 S

From the yellow print, cut:
3 CC
1 DD

From the orange-and-black dot fabric, cut:
1V

From the orange-dot fabric, cut:
Letters for word "or"

From the multicolored-striped fabric, cut:
7 strips, 2½" x 42"

MAKING THE BLOCKS

1. Sew a gray tone-on-tone 1½"-wide strip to a black tone-on-tone 1½"-wide strip along the long edges. Press the seam allowances toward the black strip. Make six strip sets. From the strip sets, cut 144 segments, 1½" wide.

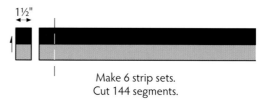

1½"

Make 6 strip sets.
Cut 144 segments.

2. Join the units from step 1 in pairs to make 72 four-patch units. Sew each unit to a gray tone-on-tone 2½" square. Press the seam allowances toward the gray square.

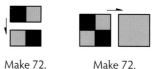

Make 72.   Make 72.

3. Join the units from step 2 in pairs to make 36 double-four-patch units. Sew each unit to a gray tone-on-tone 4½" square to make half a block. Press the seam allowances toward the gray square.

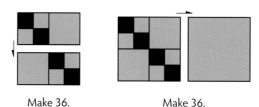

Make 36.   Make 36.

4. Join the half blocks in pairs to complete 18 blocks, measuring 8½" x 8½".

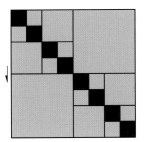

Make 18.

ASSEMBLING THE QUILT TOP

Blocks are sewn in five smaller sections to make appliquéing easier. The sections are then joined to complete the quilt top.

1. To make section A, arrange eight assorted gray 8½" squares, and four pieced blocks as shown. Sew the squares and blocks together into rows, pressing the seam allowances in opposite directions from row to row. Sew the rows together. Press the seam allowances in one direction. Referring to the quilt photo on page 24 or the quilt assembly diagram on page 28, position the two pumpkins (including stems, eyes, and mouths) along with one small bat (I) and two medium bats (H). Fuse and stitch the appliqués in place.

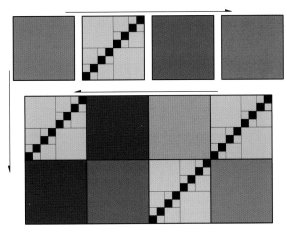

Section A assembly

2. To make section B, arrange six assorted gray 8½" squares, and two pieced blocks as shown. Sew the squares and blocks together into rows. Press the seam allowances in opposite directions from row to row. Sew the rows together. Sew section B to the bottom of section A. Referring to the quilt photo or assembly diagram, position the witch's feet, hat with hat band, spider, and one large bat (N). Fuse and stitch the appliqués in place.

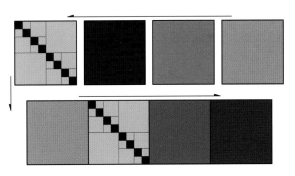

Section B assembly.
Join to bottom of section A.

3. To make section C, arrange eight assorted gray 8½" squares and four pieced blocks. Sew the squares and block together into rows. Press the seam allowances in opposite directions from row to row. Sew the rows together. Press the seam allowances in one direction. Sew section C to the bottom of section A/B. Press the seam allowances in one direction. Referring to the quilt photo or assembly diagram, position the ghost and all the pieces to complete Frankenstein. Fuse and stitch the appliqués in place. You have now completed the left side of the quilt top.

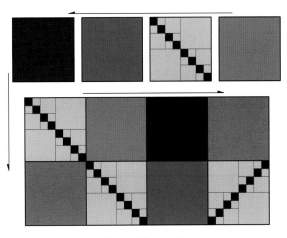

Section C assembly.
Join to bottom of section A/B.

4. To make section D, arrange eight assorted gray 8½" squares and four pieced blocks. Sew the squares and blocks together into rows. Press the seam allowances in opposite directions from row to row. Sew the rows together. Press the seam allowances in one direction. Position the words "trick or treat" and one large bat (N). Fuse and stitch the appliqués in place.

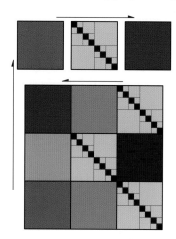

Section D assembly

5. To make section E, arrange eight assorted gray 8½" squares and four black and gray blocks. Sew the squares and blocks together into rows. Press the seam allowances in opposite directions from row to row. Sew the rows together. Press the seam allowances in one direction. Position the moon and stars. Fuse and stitch the appliqués in place.

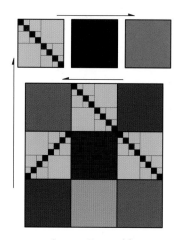

Section E assembly

6. Sew section E to the bottom of section D. Press the seam allowances in one direction. Position the skeleton head, bones, eyes, nose and mouth. Fuse and stitch the appliqués in place. This completes the right side of the quilt top.

7. Sew the right and left sides together. Position one large bat (N) and one small bat (I). Fuse and stitch the appliqués in place.

Quilt assembly

8. Referring to "Decorative Stitching" on page 9, use a decorative stitch and black thread to stitch the spider legs and the web dangling him from the witch's hat. Use a machine double stitch or hand embroidery to stitch Frankenstein's mouth, the ghost's mouth, and segment lines on the pumpkins.

FINISHING THE QUILT

Refer to "Finishing" on page 9 as needed.

1. Layer the quilt top, batting, and backing; baste. Quilt as desired. I machine stitched a linear echo, sort of a large stipple design in lines, all over the quilt. I also stitched around each appliqué piece to anchor it and give definition.

2. Using the orange-and-black 2½"-wide strips, sew the binding to the quilt.

3. Sew on two black buttons for the spider's eyes.

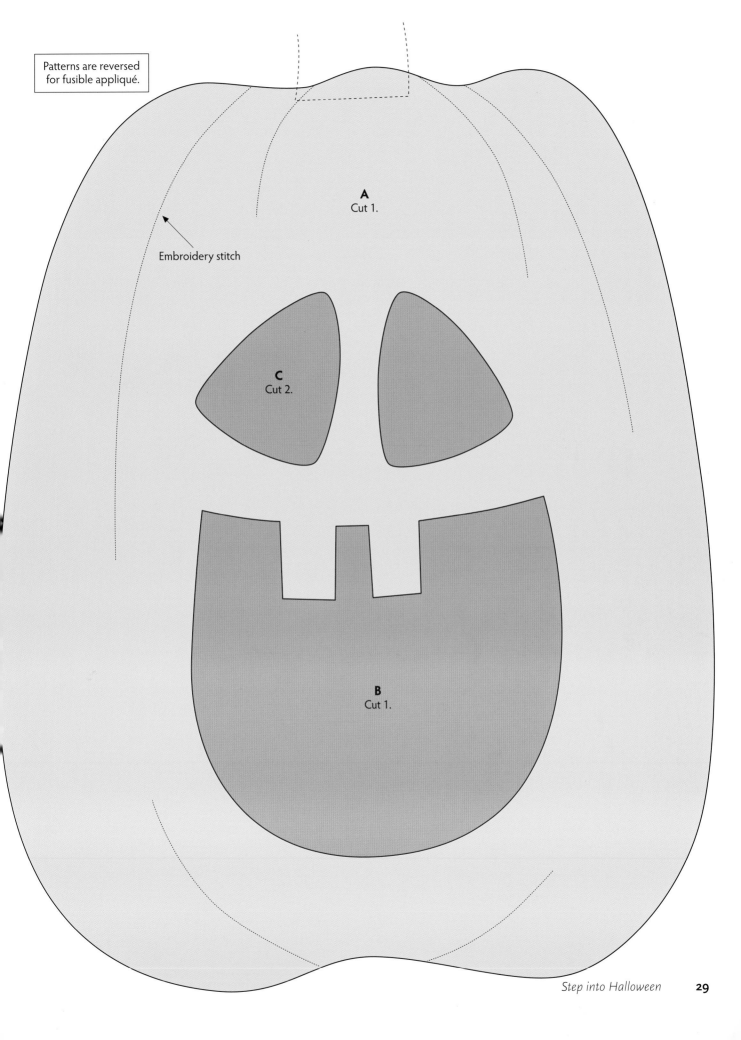

Patterns are reversed
for fusible appliqué.

A
Cut 1.

Embroidery stitch

C
Cut 2.

B
Cut 1.

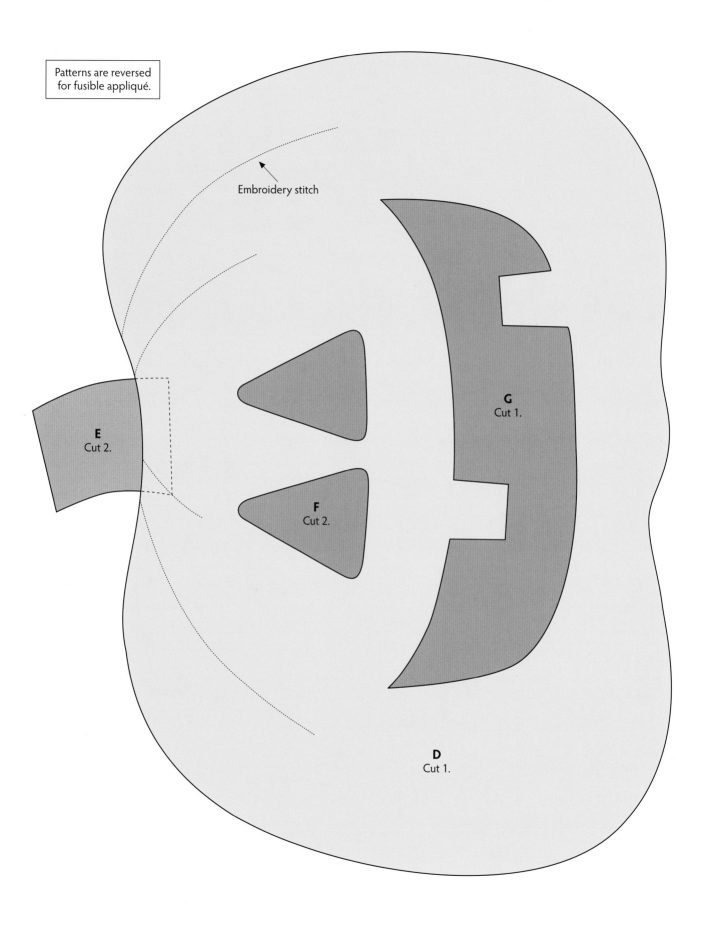

Patterns are reversed
for fusible appliqué.

Embroidery stitch

E
Cut 2.

G
Cut 1.

F
Cut 2.

D
Cut 1.

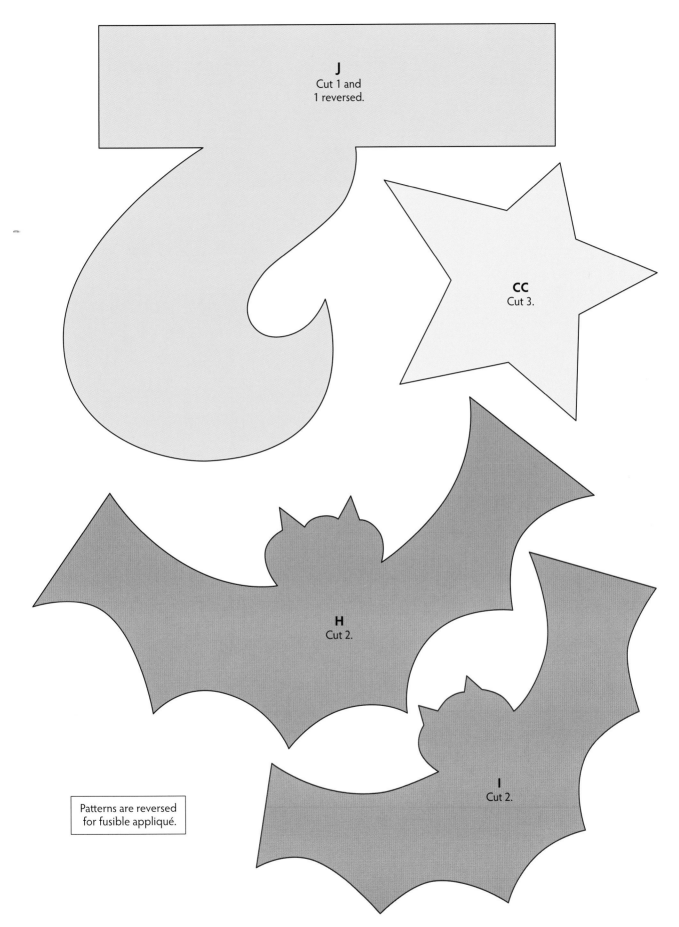

J
Cut 1 and
1 reversed.

CC
Cut 3.

H
Cut 2.

I
Cut 2.

Patterns are reversed
for fusible appliqué.

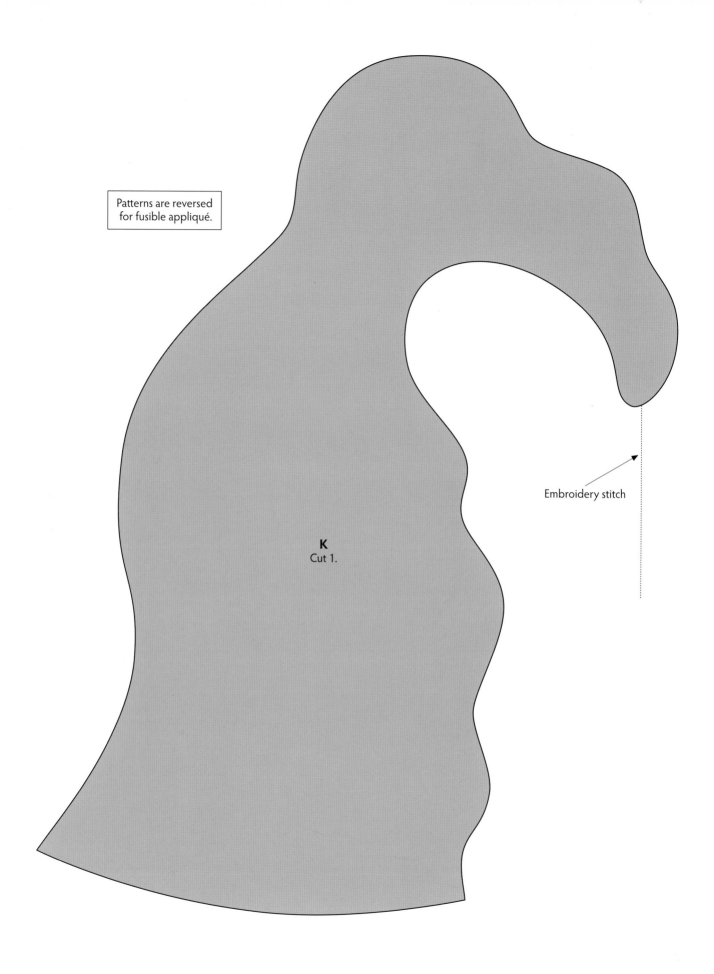

Patterns are reversed
for fusible appliqué.

Embroidery stitch

K
Cut 1.

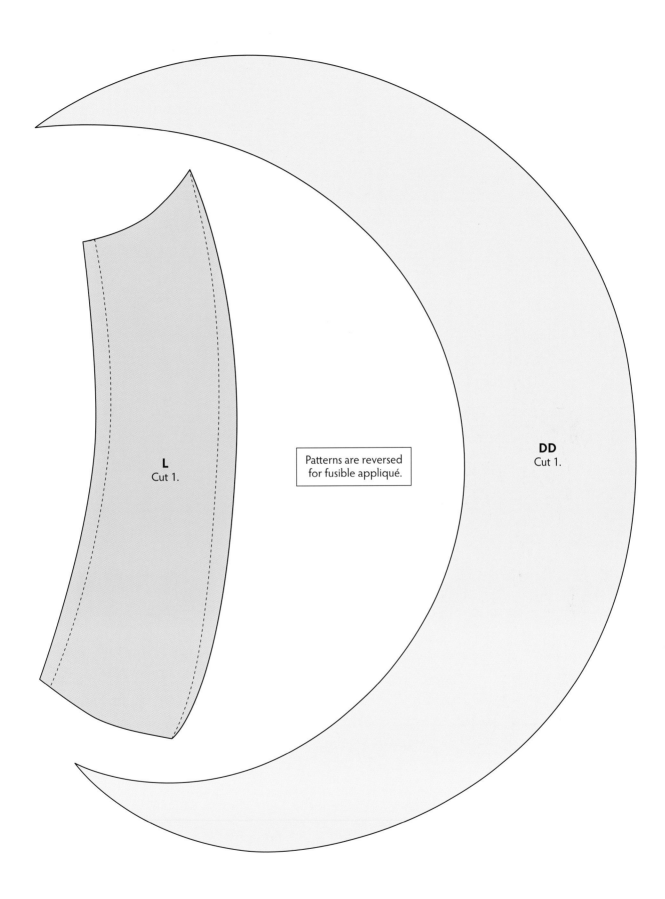

L
Cut 1.

Patterns are reversed
for fusible appliqué.

DD
Cut 1.

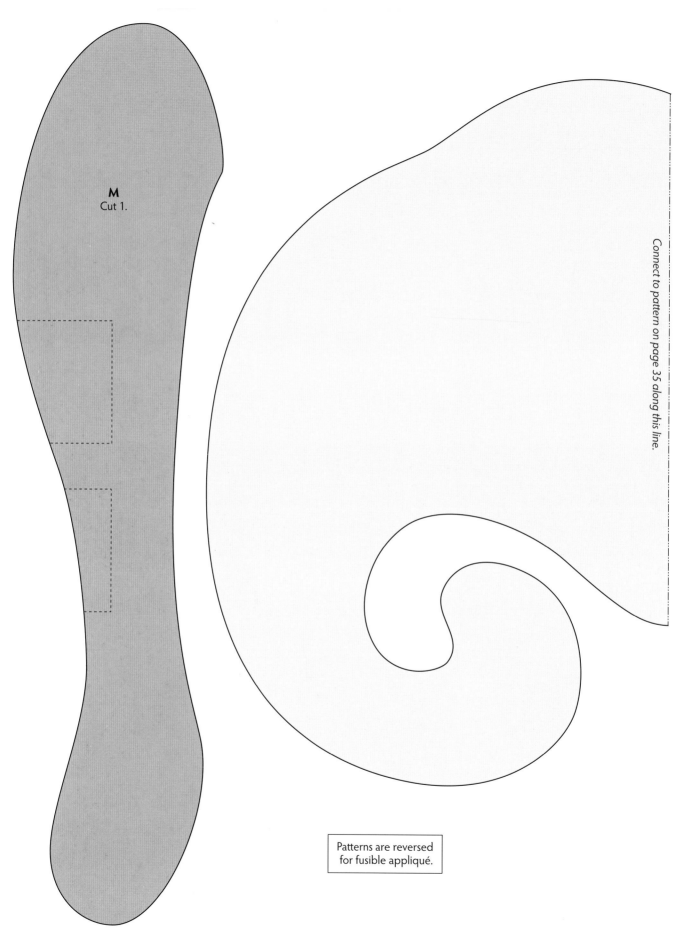

M
Cut 1.

Connect to pattern on page 35 along this line.

Patterns are reversed
for fusible appliqué.

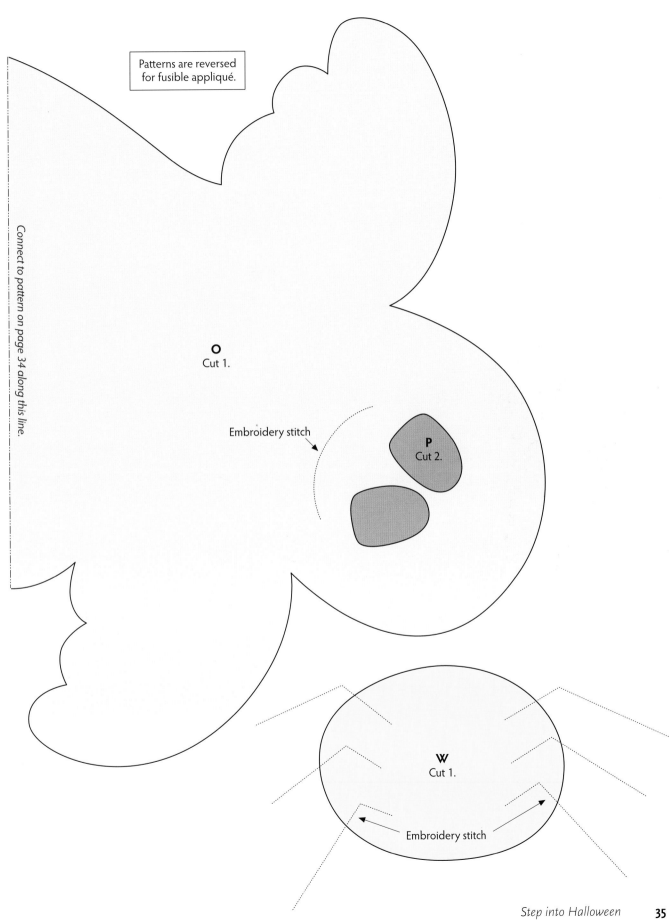

Patterns are reversed
for fusible appliqué.

Connect to pattern on page 34 along this line.

O
Cut 1.

Embroidery stitch

P
Cut 2.

W
Cut 1.

Embroidery stitch

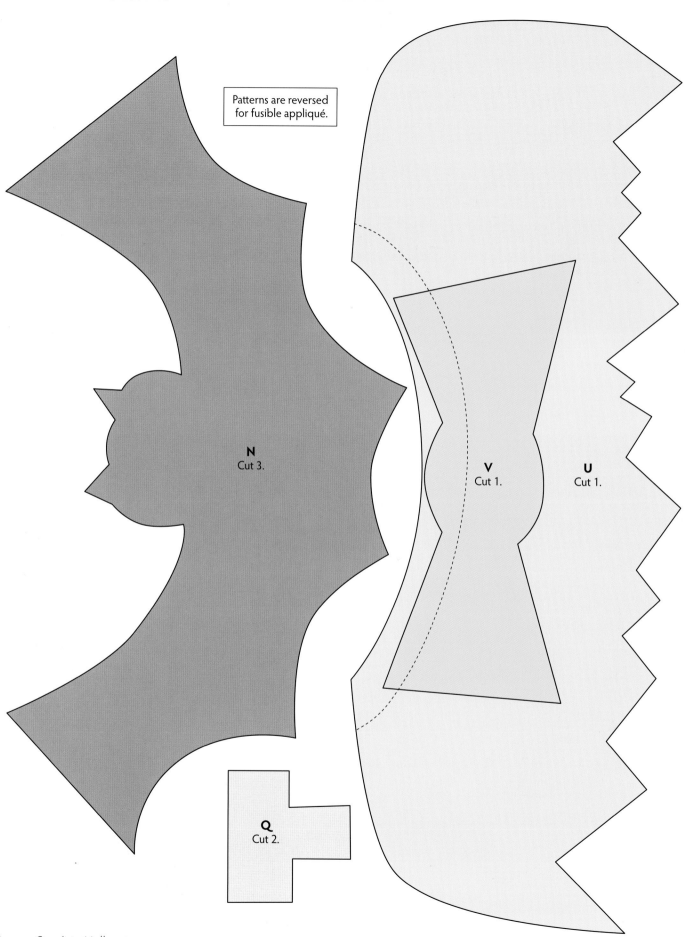

Patterns are reversed
for fusible appliqué.

N
Cut 3.

V
Cut 1.

U
Cut 1.

Q
Cut 2.

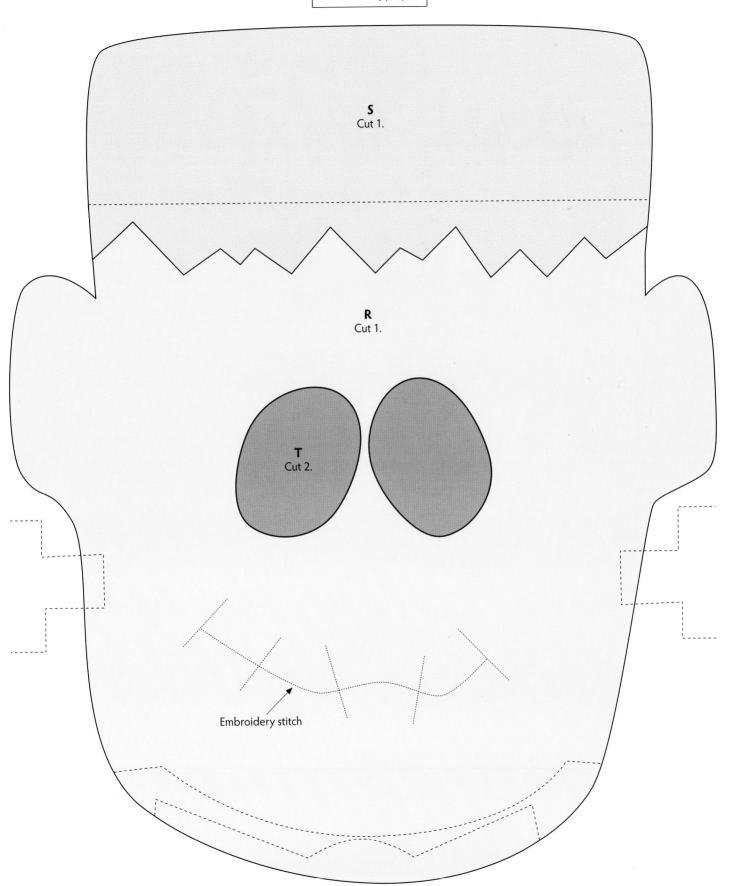

Patterns are reversed
for fusible appliqué.

S
Cut 1.

R
Cut 1.

T
Cut 2.

Embroidery stitch

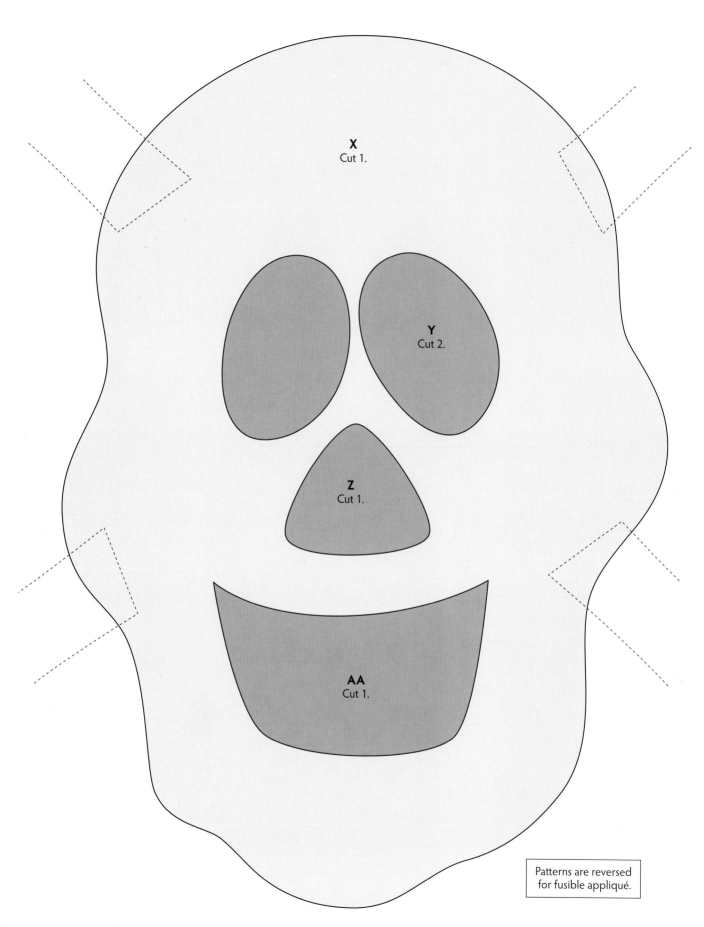

X
Cut 1.

Y
Cut 2.

Z
Cut 1.

AA
Cut 1.

Patterns are reversed
for fusible appliqué.

Cut 1.

Cut 1.

Cut 3.

Cut 3.

Cut 1.

Patterns are reversed for fusible appliqué.

Cut 1.

Cut 1.

Cut 1.

BB
Cut 4.

Designed, pieced, and quilted by Geralyn Powers

FINISHED QUILT: 57½" x 67½" ▪ FINISHED BLOCK: 9" x 9"

Aunt Rachael's Garden

I grew up in a small, closely knit community and lived next door to Aunt Rachael. She wasn't really my aunt, but my grandmother's cousin. She had been a widow for over 40 years and her life was her garden—a quintessential English garden in a hot, dry corner of New Mexico! She planted row after row of colorful flowers, including hollyhocks, snapdragons, roses, daffodils, sweet peas, and irises to name only a few. It was a splendid array of color in a desert oasis and began a love of flowers very early in my life. This quilt was inspired by her garden.

MATERIALS

Yardage is based on 42"-wide fabric. Fat quarters measure approximately 18" x 21".

1¾ yards light-blue print for outer border and binding*

*If desired, you'll have enough fabric left over to cut some squares for use in the blocks (as shown in the photo).

1⅜ yards of blue-on-white mini-dot fabric for appliqué background

⅞ yard royal-blue tone-on-tone fabric for blocks and inner border

⅛ yard *each* of two green prints for leaves

6 fat quarters of coordinating blue prints for blocks and flowers

3 fat quarters of coordinating red prints for blocks and flowers

3 fat quarters of coordinating pink prints for blocks and flowers

4¼ yards of fabric for backing

61" x 71" piece of batting

1 yard of lightweight fusible web for appliqués

Thread in coordinating colors for appliqués

CUTTING

All measurements include ¼"-wide seam allowance. Cut all strips across the width of the fabric unless otherwise indicated.

The appliqué patterns for pieces A–F are on page 44. For information on preparing and cutting pieces for fusible appliqué, refer to "Fusible Appliqué" on page 8.

From the blue fat quarters, cut *a total of:*
40 squares, 5" x 5"

From the pink and red fat quarters, cut *a total of:*
40 squares, 5" x 5"

From the royal-blue tone-on-tone fabric, cut:
4 strips, 2" x 42"; crosscut into 80 squares, 2" x 2"
8 strips, 2" x 42"

From the blue-on-white mini-dot fabric, cut *on the lengthwise grain:*
2 strips, 8½" x 45½"

From the light-blue print, cut:
7 strips, 5" x 42"
7 strips, 2½" x 42"

Continued on page 42

From the remainder of the blue fat quarters, cut:
1 A
1 B
2 C
4 F

From the remainder of the pink fat quarters, cut:
1 A
1 B
2 C
2 F

From the remainder of the red fat quarters, cut:
1 A
1 B
4 F

From *each* green fat quarter, cut:
5 D (10 total)
5 E (10 total)

MAKING THE BLOCKS

1. Referring to "Folded-Triangle Units" on page 7, sew a royal-blue 2" square to one corner of a blue print 5" square. Press the seam allowances away from the corner. Make 40 blue units. Repeat with a royal-blue 2" square on a pink (or red) print 5" square. Press the seam allowances toward the corner. Make 40 pink (or red) units.

Make 40.   Make 40.

2. Join four assorted blue units from step 1, with the triangles on the outer corners. The block should measure 9½" x 9½". Make 10 blue

blocks. Press the seam allowances as indicated. Repeat to make 10 pink (or red) blocks.

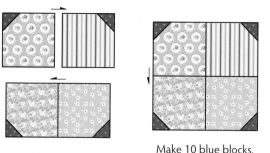

Make 10 blue blocks.

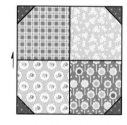

Make 10 pink blocks.

ASSEMBLING THE QUILT TOP

1. Arrange the blocks in four rows of five blocks each, alternating pink (or red) and blue blocks from row to row. Placing the blocks on a large flat surface or design wall will help in arranging the colors. Sew the blocks together into rows. Press the seam allowances in opposite directions from row to row. Sew the rows together. Press the seam allowances in one direction.

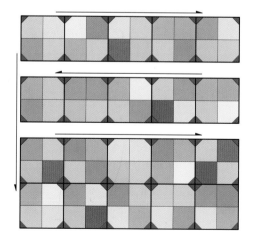

2. Join the royal-blue 2" x 42" strips end to end to make one long strip. Cut four 2" x 45½" strips. Sew the strips to each long edge of the 8½" x 45½" appliqué background strips. Press the seam allowances toward the blue strips. Lay the appliqué strips at the top and bottom of the quilt. Arrange the leaves and flowers on the strips, aligning the flowers and leaves with the block seams. Make sure the appliqués are away from the top and bottom seam allowances. Fuse and stitch the appliqués in place. Sew the appliquéd 8½" x 45½" strips to the top and bottom of the quilt.

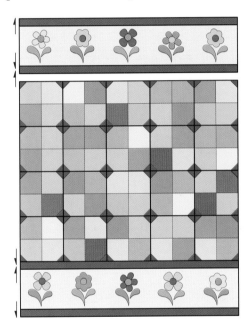

Quilt assembly

3. From the joined royal-blue strip, cut two 2" x 58½" strips and sew them to opposite sides of the quilt. Press.

4. Join the light-blue 5" x 42" strips end to end to make one long strip. Cut two 5" x 58½" strips and sew them to opposite sides of the quilt. Press the seam allowances toward the borders. Cut two 5" x 57½" strips and sew them to the top and bottom of the quilt. Press.

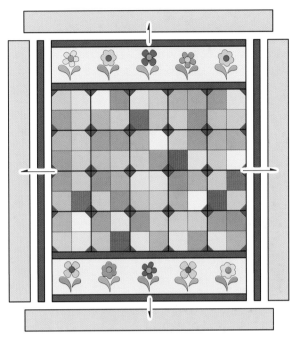

Border assembly

FINISHING THE QUILT

Refer to "Finishing" on page 9 as needed.

1. Layer the quilt top, batting, and backing; baste. Quilt as desired. I machine quilted in the ditch on all seams except the center block. I quilted a leaf design on the dark-blue borders and an allover floral pattern on the blocks and outer border. The appliqué background is quilted with swirls, plus stitching around all flowers for definition.
2. Using the light-blue 2½"-wide strips, sew the binding to the quilt.

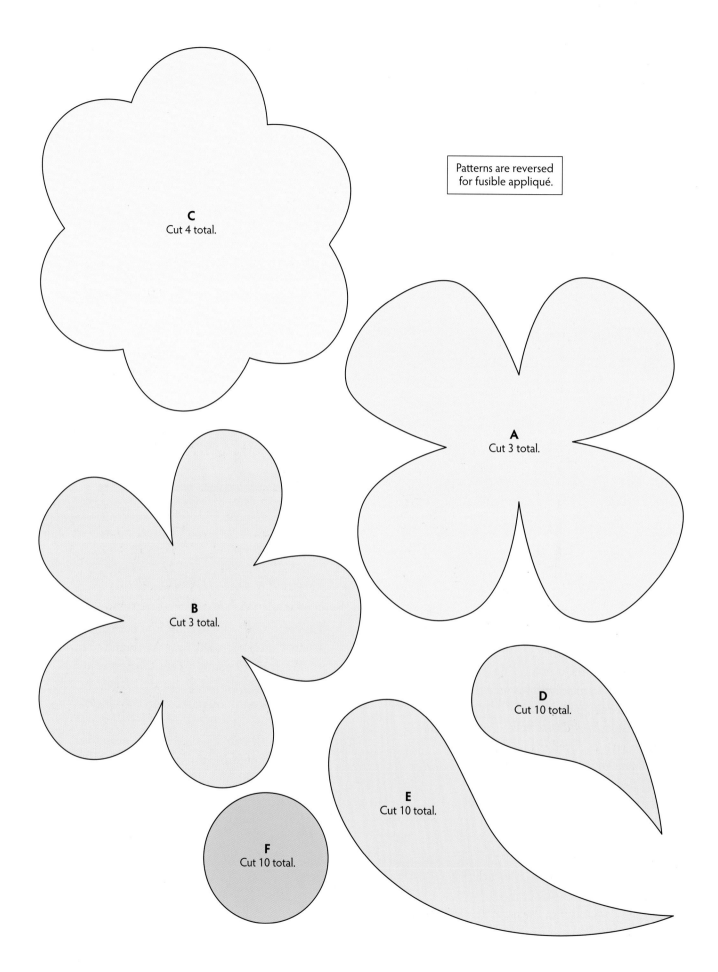

C
Cut 4 total.

Patterns are reversed
for fusible appliqué.

A
Cut 3 total.

B
Cut 3 total.

D
Cut 10 total.

E
Cut 10 total.

F
Cut 10 total.

Gingermania

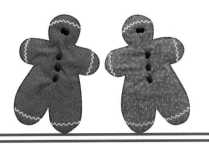

Few things are more delightful during the Christmas season than the sight and smell of freshly baked gingerbread. The aroma and colors warm the heart, hence "Gingermania" could be an issue at my house all year long. This quilt was inspired by the memory, nostalgia, and taste of old-fashioned gingerbread cookies—and a love for holiday decorating!

MATERIALS

Yardage is based on 42"-wide fabric. Fat quarters measure approximately 18" x 21".

2 yards of dark-brown print for inner borders, outer borders, and binding

⅝ yard of cream solid for embroidered and gingerbread-men panels

5 fat quarters of dark-brown prints for blocks

5 fat quarters of red prints for blocks

3 fat quarters of pink prints for blocks

3 fat quarters of tan prints for blocks

4 fat quarters of green prints for blocks

5 fat quarters of medium-brown prints for blocks and appliqués

4¼ yards of fabric for backing

2 yards golden-brown jumbo rickrack and matching thread

Cream thread for decorative stitching, and black thread for appliqués

67" x 70" piece of batting

20 black buttons for eyes, ¼" diameter

30 brown buttons for gingerbread men, ⅜" diameter*

1 yard lightweight fusible web for appliqués

Size 12 pearl cotton in dark brown for embroidery

See "Resources" on page 80 for "raisin" buttons.

CUTTING

All measurements include ¼"-wide seam allowances. Cut all strips across the width of fabric unless otherwise instructed.

The appliqué patterns for pieces A and B are on page 51. For information on preparing and cutting pieces for fusible appliqué, refer to "Fusible Appliqué" on page 8.

From each of the 25 fat quarters, cut:

1 strip, 1¾" x 20"; crosscut into:
    2 rectangles, 1¾" x 2½" (25 pairs total)
    2 rectangles, 1¾" x 5" (25 pairs total)

2 strips, 2¼" x 20"; crosscut into:
    2 rectangles, 2¼" x 5" (25 pairs total)
    2 rectangles, 2¼" x 8½" (25 pairs total)

2 strips, 1½" x 20"; crosscut into:
    2 strips, 1½" x 8½" (25 pairs total)
    2 strips, 1½" x 10½" (25 pairs total)

1 square, 2½" x 2½" (25 total)

From remaining portions of the medium-brown prints, cut:

5 A

5 B

From the cream solid, cut:

2 strips, 8½" x 42"; crosscut into:
    1 rectangle, 8½" x 18½"
    1 rectangle, 8½" x 28½"

Continued on page 47

The block contains embroidered text: Flour, Sugar, Ginger, Cinnamon, Nutmeg, Allspice, Raisins, Molasses

Designed, pieced, and quilted by Geralyn Powers; embroidered by Mary Van Syoc

FINISHED QUILT: 63½" x 66½" ▪ FINISHED BLOCK: 10" x 10"

From the dark-brown print, cut:
4 strips, 1½" x 42"; crosscut into:
    2 strips, 1½" x 28½"
    2 strips, 1½" x 18½"
    4 strips, 1½" x 10½"
6 strips, 3½" x 42"
2 strips, 10½" x 42"
7 strips, 2½" x 42"

MAKING THE BLOCKS

1. Choose two 1¾" x 2½" rectangles and two 1¾" x 5" rectangles of the same color, and one contrasting 2½" square. Sew them together as shown. Press the seam allowances away from the center square. Make 25 units.

Make 25.

2. Choose two 2¼" x 5" rectangles and two 2¼" x 8½" rectangles of the same color, yet different from the rectangles in step 1. Sew the 2¼" x 5" rectangles to opposite sides of the unit, and the 2¼" x 8½" rectangles to the top and bottom. Press the seam allowances away from the center square. Make 25 units.

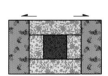 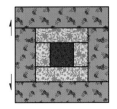

Make 25.

3. Choose two 1½" x 8½" strips and two 1½" x 10½" strips of the same color, yet different from the rectangles in steps 1 and 2. Sew the 1½" x 8½" strips to opposite sides of the unit, and the 1½" x 10½" strips to the top and bottom to complete the block. Press the seam

allowances away from the center square. The block should measure 10½" x 10½". Make 25 blocks.

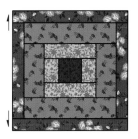

Make 25 blocks.

MAKING THE EMBROIDERED AND APPLIQUÉD PANELS

1. To make the embroidered panel, sew two dark-brown print 1½" x 18½" strips to opposite sides of the cream 8½" x 18½" rectangle. Press the seam allowances toward the dark-brown strips. Sew two dark-brown print 1½" x 10½" strips to the top and bottom of the unit. Press the seam allowances toward the brown strips. Trace the words (page 50) onto the cream rectangle and hand embroider them using one strand of dark-brown pearl cotton and a stem stitch (see "Decorative Stitching" on page 9).

Flour
Sugar
Ginger
Cinnamon
Nutmeg
Allspice
Raisins
Molasses

ASSEMBLING THE QUILT TOP

1. Arrange the blocks in six rows, placing the embroidery panel and gingerbread-men panel as shown. Rotate the blocks so the longest strips of the blocks alternate horizontally and vertically from block to block. Sew the rows of five blocks together. Sew the short rows of blocks together before joining them with the panels. Press the seam allowances in opposite directions from row to row. Sew the rows together. Press the seam allowances in one direction.

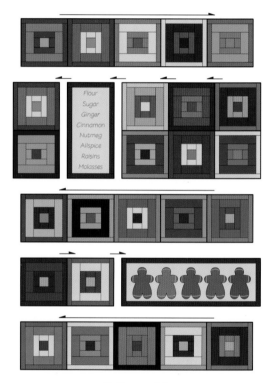

Quilt assembly

2. To make the gingerbread-men panel, sew the dark-brown 1½" x 28½" strips to the top and bottom of the cream 8½" x 28½" rectangle. Press the seam allowances toward the dark-brown strips. Sew the remaining dark-brown 1½" x 10½" strips to opposite sides of the rectangle. Press the seam allowances toward the dark-brown strips.

3. Arrange the small gingerbread men horizontally on the panel, and fuse them in place. For frosting, use cream-colored thread and a decorative stitch on your machine that looks similar to rickrack. Stitch frosting on the legs, arms, and head of the gingerbread men (see "Decorative Stitching"). Use black thread to stitch the appliqués in place.

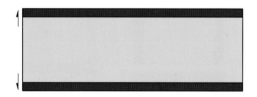

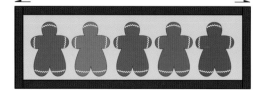

2. Join the dark-brown 3½" x 42" border strips end to end to make one long strip. Cut one 3½" x 60½" strip and sew it to the right side of the quilt. Press the seam allowances toward the border. Cut two 3½" x 53¼" strips and sew them to the top and bottom of the quilt. Press the seam allowances toward the border.

3. Join two dark-brown 10½" x 42" border strips end to end to make one long strip. Cut one 10½" x 66½" strip. Arrange five large gingerbread men vertically on this strip, positioning

them toward the left side of the strip so there is room for the jumbo rickrack. Tilt them left and right for fun. Fuse them in place. Stitch the frosting as for the small gingerbread men. Stitch the appliqués in place. Sew the appliquéd panel to the left side of the quilt. Press the seam allowances toward the panel.

FINISHING THE QUILT

Refer to "Finishing" on page 9 as needed.

1. Layer the quilt top, batting, and backing (pieced horizontally); baste. Quilt as desired. I used an overall, large stipple design on the blocks and borders, and a smaller stipple design on the appliqué backgrounds.

2. After quilting, pin or glue baste the golden-brown jumbo rickrack onto the left, appliquéd border. Put the free-motion quilting foot on your machine and lower the feed dogs. Using thread that matches the rickrack, stitch along the curves next to the edge. Stitch down each side of the rickrack. The matching thread "sinks" into the rickrack and your stitches will hardly show.

3. Using the dark-brown 2½"-wide strips, sew the binding to the quilt.

4. On each gingerbread man, sew two black buttons for eyes, and three "raisin" buttons, referring to the photo on page 46 as needed.

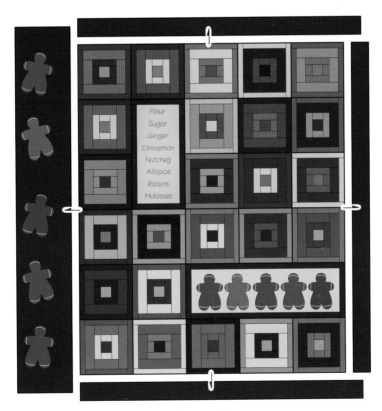

Border assembly

Flour Sugar
Ginger
Cinnamon
Nutmeg
Allspice
Raisins
Molasses

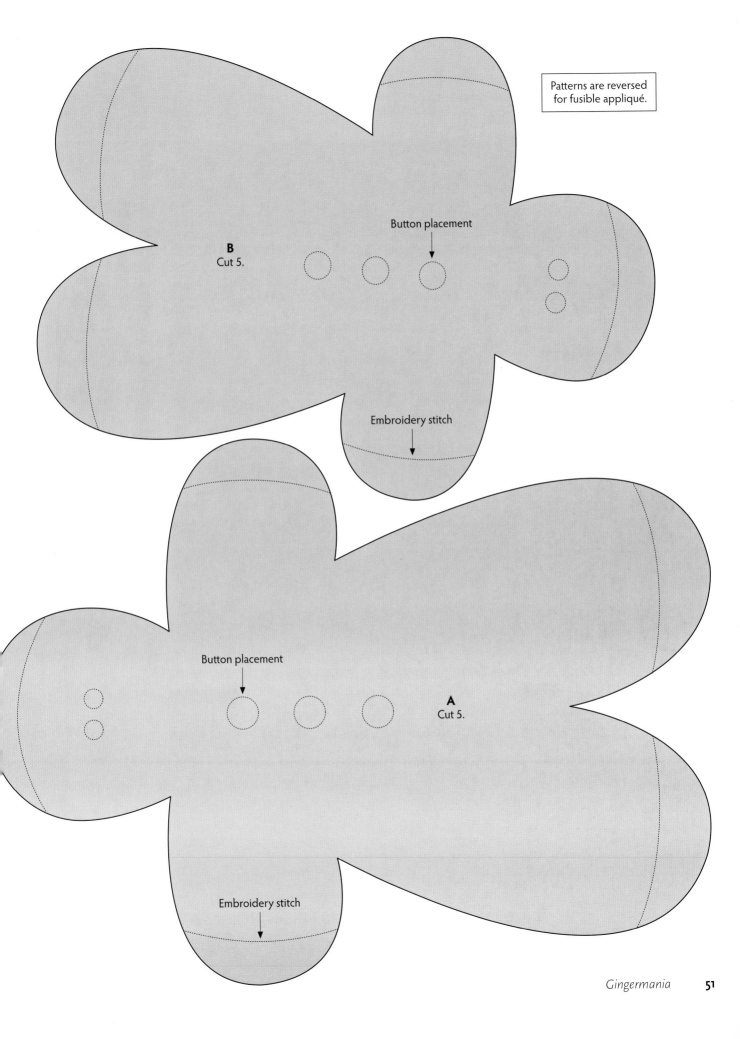

Patterns are reversed
for fusible appliqué.

B
Cut 5.

Button placement

Embroidery stitch

Button placement

A
Cut 5.

Embroidery stitch

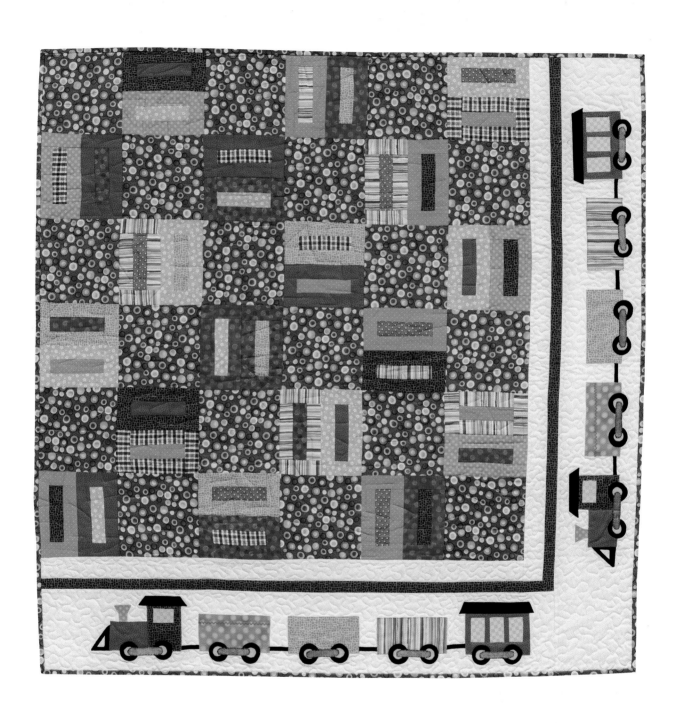

Designed, pieced, and quilted by Geralyn Powers
FINISHED QUILT: 44¾" x 44¾" ▪ FINISHED BLOCK: 6" x 6"

Jordan's Train

This quilt was inspired by a little boy who from a very early age loved playing with his trains. He was so enthralled; it was a joy for everyone to watch him. The trains are a whimsical reminder that childhood is precious and fleeting.

MATERIALS

Yardage is based on 42"-wide fabric. Fat quarters measure approximately 18" x 21". Fat eighths measure approximately 9" x 21".

1⅓ yards of white solid for first and third borders
1 yard of bright blue print for blocks and binding
⅛ yard of blue tone-on-tone fabric for second border
8 fat quarters of coordinating colors for blocks and appliqués
1 fat eighth of gray solid for wheels
1 fat eighth of black solid for wheels and train cars
1 fat eighth of yellow tone-on-tone fabric for windows and wheels
3¼ yards of fabric for backing
49" x 49" piece of batting
1½ yards of lightweight fusible web for appliqués
Thread in coordinating colors for appliqués

CUTTING

All measurements include ¼"-wide seam allowances. Cut all strips across the width of fabric unless otherwise instructed.

The appliqué patterns for pieces A–O are on pages 56 and 57. For information on preparing and cutting pieces for fusible appliqué, refer to "Fusible Appliqué" on page 8.

From *each* of the eight coordinating fat quarters, cut:
14 rectangles, 1½" x 4½" (112 total; 4 are extra)
10 rectangles, 1½" x 3½" (80 total; 8 are extra)

From the bright blue print, cut:
3 strips, 6½" x 42"; crosscut into 18 squares, 6½" x 6½"
5 strips, 2½" x 42"

From the white solid, cut *on the lengthwise grain*:
1 strip, 2" x 36½"
1 strip, 2" x 38"
1 strip, 6½" x 38¾"
1 strip, 6½" x 44¾"

From the blue tone-on-tone fabric, cut:
1 strip, 1¼" x 38"
1 strip, 1¼" x 38¾"

From the remainder of the coordinating fat quarters, using colors of your choice, cut:
2 A
2 B
2 D
6 K
2 M

From the white solid, cut:
2 F

Continued on page 54

From the black solid, cut:
20 H
8 L
2 C
2 N
2 E

From the gray solid, cut:
10 J

From the yellow tone-on-tone fabric, cut:
20 I
2 G
6 O

MAKING THE BLOCKS

1. Choose two 1½" x 3½" rectangles and two 1½" x 4½" rectangles of the same color, and one contrasting 1½" x 4½" rectangle. Sew them together as shown. Press the seam allowances away from the center rectangle. Make 36 units.

Make 36.

2. Choosing two different colored units from step 1, sew the units into pairs along the long edges. The block should measure 6½" x 6½". Make 18 blocks.

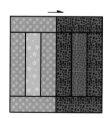

Make 18.

ASSEMBLING THE QUILT TOP

1. Arrange the blocks and bright blue 6½" squares into six rows of six blocks each, rotating the pieced blocks from row to row as shown. Sew the blocks and squares together into rows. Press the seam allowances toward the bright blue squares. Sew the rows together. Press the seam allowances in one direction.

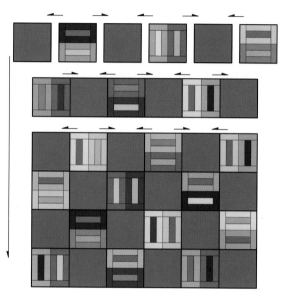

Quilt assembly

2. Arrange the trains on the white solid 6½" x 38¾", and 6½" x 44¾" outer-border strips, keeping the pieces the required distance from the ends, as indicated below. Fuse and stitch the appliqués in place. I also added a decorative rickrack stitch to the second car (see "Decorative Stitching" on page 9). Feel free to embellish the cars as you wish, adding a child's name to personalize the quilt.

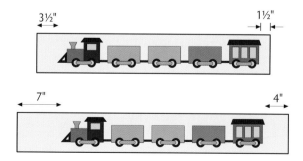

3. Sew the white 2" x 36½" border strip to the bottom of the quilt. Sew the white 2" x 38" border strip to the right side of the quilt. Press all seam allowances away from the white border strips.

4. Sew the blue 1¼" x 38" border strip to the bottom of the quilt. Sew the blue 1¼" x 38¾" border strip to the right side of the quilt. Press all seam allowances away from the white border strips.

5. Sew the 6½" x 38¾" train border to the bottom of quilt. Sew the 6½" x 44¾" train border to the right side of quilt. Press all seam allowances away from the white border strips.

FINISHING THE QUILT

Refer to "Finishing" on page 9 as needed.

1. Layer the quilt top, batting, and backing (pieced horizontally); baste. Quilt as desired. I used an overall, straight-line maze design on the blocks and a small stipple design on the appliqué background. I stitched around each train car to anchor it and give it definition.

2. Using the bright blue 2½"-wide strips, sew the binding to the quilt.

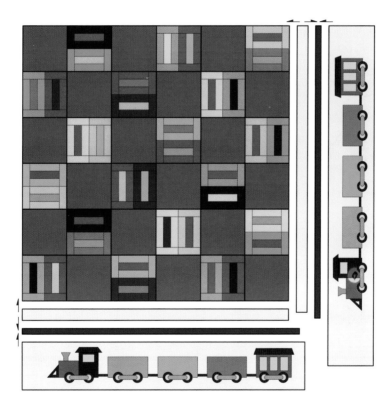

Border assembly

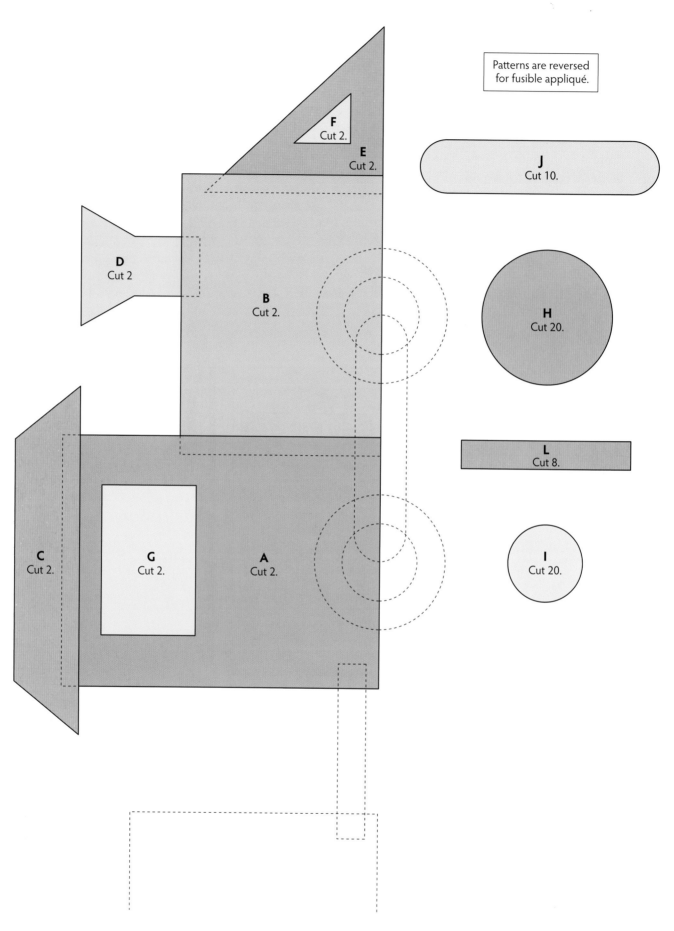

Patterns are reversed for fusible appliqué.

F Cut 2.

E Cut 2.

J Cut 10.

D Cut 2

B Cut 2.

H Cut 20.

L Cut 8.

C Cut 2.

G Cut 2.

A Cut 2.

I Cut 20.

Patterns are reversed
for fusible appliqué.

N
Cut 2.

O
Cut 6.

M
Cut 2.

K
Cut 6.

Designed, pieced, and quilted by Geralyn Powers
FINISHED QUILT: 68½" x 78½" ▪ FINISHED BLOCK: 9" x 9"

Freedom Waves

Rich patriotic colors along with traditional blocks are used in this heartwarming quilt, designed to keep or give away. It's a great project to bring out during patriotic celebrations, or to leave out all year. And giving a handmade quilt to a veteran is a great way to express appreciation for military service.

MATERIALS

Yardage is based on 42"-wide fabric. Fat quarters measure approximately 18" x 21".

1⅝ yards of beige print for appliqué background
⅜ yard *each* of 8 assorted red prints for blocks, appliqué, and outer border
¼ yard *each* of 6 assorted navy- and soldier-blue prints for blocks and appliqués
¼ yard *each* of 6 assorted beige prints for blocks
1¼ yards of navy-blue print for inner border, corner blocks, and binding
1 fat quarter of green print for vines and leaves
10" x 10" square of gold print for stars
10" x 10" square of brown print for flag poles
4½ yards of fabric for backing (pieced horizontally)
72" x 82" piece of batting
2 yards of lightweight fusible web for appliqués
Thread in coordinating colors for appliqués

CUTTING

All measurements include ¼"-wide seam allowances. Cut all strips across the width of fabric unless otherwise instructed.

The appliqué patterns for pieces A–H are on pages 62 and 63. For information on preparing and cutting pieces for fusible appliqué, refer to "Fusible Appliqué" on page 8.

From *each* red print, cut
1 strip, 6" x 42" (8 total)
3 strips, 2" x 42"; crosscut into 12 rectangles, 2" x 9½" (96 total)

From *each* navy- or soldier-blue print, cut:
3 strips, 2" x 42"; crosscut into 10 rectangles, 2" x 9½" (60 total)

From *each* beige print, cut:
3 strips, 2" x 42"; crosscut into 10 rectangles, 2" x 9½" (60 total)

From the beige print for appliqué background, cut *on the lengthwise grain*;
1 strip, 10½" x 54½"

From the navy-blue print, cut:
4 squares, 6" x 6"
8 strips, 2" x 42"
8 strips, 2½" x 42"

From the remainder of the assorted red prints, cut:
5 A

From the remainder of the assorted blue prints, cut:
5 B

Continued on page 60

From the green print, cut:
1 F and 1 reversed
1 G
1 H
29 D

From the gold print, cut:
7 E

From the brown print, cut:
5 C

MAKING THE BLOCKS

Choose six 2" x 9½" strips in assorted colors. Join the strips along the long edges. Press the seam allowances in one direction. The block should measure 9½" x 9½". Make 36 blocks.

Make 36.

ASSEMBLING THE QUILT TOP

1. Arrange the five flags on the beige 10½" x 54½" strip, centering one flag in the middle, and two flags on each side. Position the vines, adding 29 leaves and 7 stars, and taking care to keep all pieces away from the seam allowance. Fuse and stitch the appliqués in place.

2. Arrange the blocks in six rows of six blocks each, alternating the direction of the blocks from row to row. Place the appliquéd panel below the first row. Sew the blocks together into rows. Press the seam allowances in opposite directions from row to row. Sew the rows of blocks and the appliquéd panel together. Press the seam allowances in one direction.

Quilt assembly

3. Join the navy-blue 2" x 42" strips end to end to make one long strip. Cut two 2" x 64½" strips and sew them to opposite sides of the quilt. Press the seam allowances toward the blue strips. Cut two 2" x 57½" strips and sew them to the top and bottom of the quilt. Press the seam allowances toward the blue strips.

4. Cut the red 6" x 42" strips into varying strip lengths, approximately 6" x 12", 6" x 14", and 6" x 16". They do not need to be exact. Sew the strips together end to end, varying the color placement, to make one long strip. Cut two 6" x 67½" strips and sew them to opposite sides of the quilt. Press the seam allowances toward the blue strips. Cut two 6" x 57½" strips, and sew navy-blue 6" squares to opposite ends of each strip. Sew the strips to the top and bottom of the quilt. Press the seam allowances toward the blue strips.

FINISHING THE QUILT

Refer to "Finishing" on page 9 as needed.

1. Layer the quilt top, batting, and backing (pieced horizontally); baste. Quilt as desired. I used an overall, large meandering design with stars, and a small stipple design on the appliqué background. I stitched around the flags to anchor them and give them definition.
2. Using the navy-blue 2½"-wide strips, sew the binding to the quilt.

Border assembly

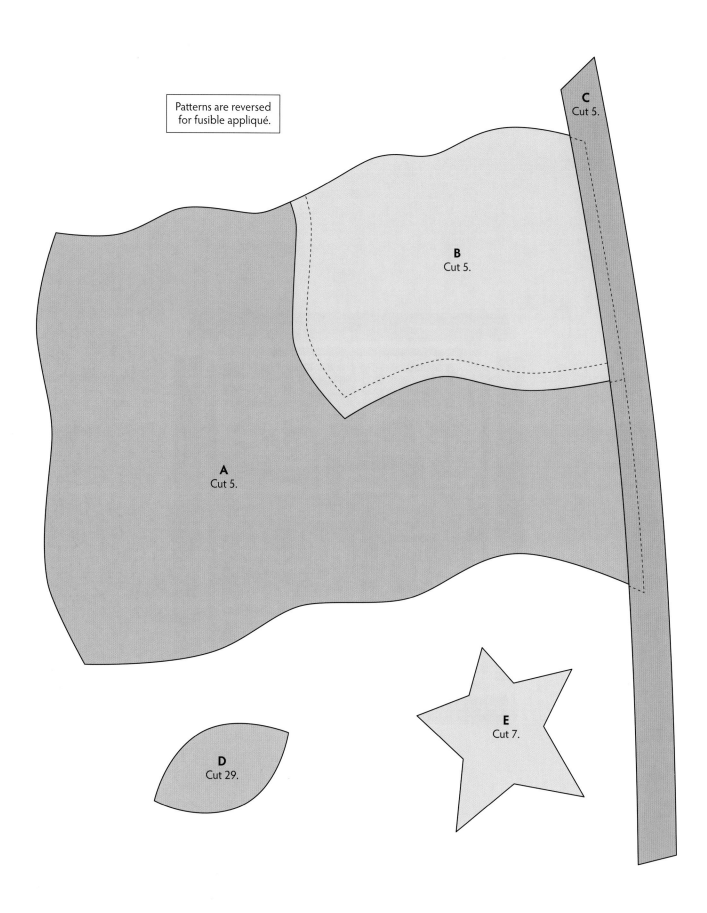

Patterns are reversed
for fusible appliqué.

C
Cut 5.

B
Cut 5.

A
Cut 5.

D
Cut 29.

E
Cut 7.

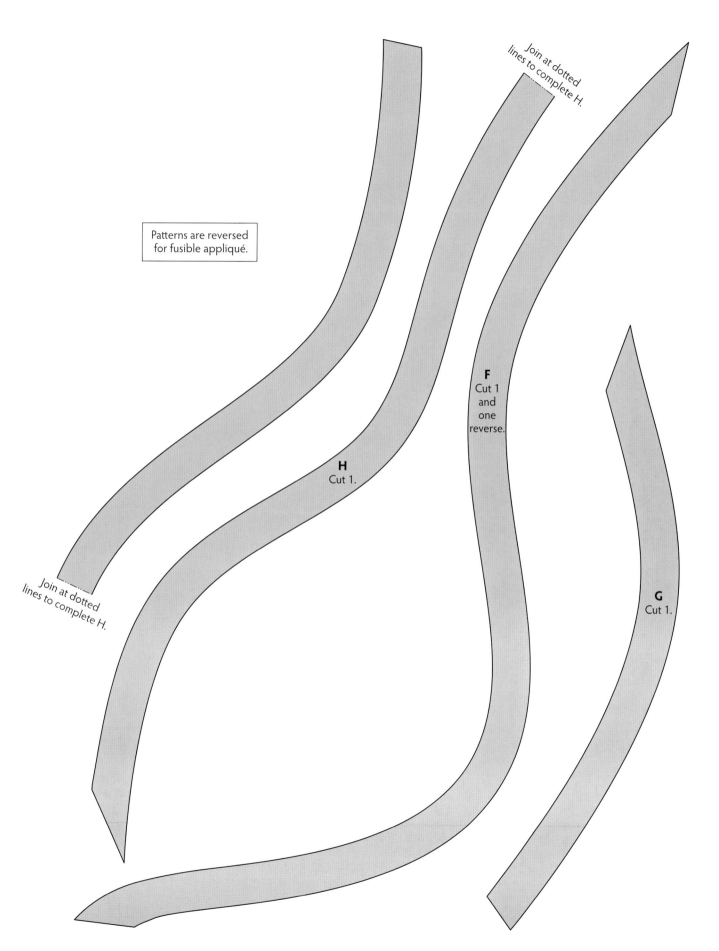

Join at dotted
lines to complete H.

Patterns are reversed
for fusible appliqué.

H
Cut 1.

F
Cut 1
and
one
reverse.

G
Cut 1.

Join at dotted
lines to complete H.

Designed, pieced, and quilted by Geralyn Powers

FINISHED QUILT: 58½" x 64½" ▪ FINISHED BLOCK: 8" x 8"

Grandma's Legacy

My grandmothers were very industrious women and both were very creative. Each had a drawer full of colorful aprons. One grandmother had the most fascinating collection of aprons that she had made, including many different designs, styles, and colors. My other grandmother had her work aprons and her Sunday apron, also handmade. This quilt was created in memory of two grand women whose lives shaped mine by their constant service to their families and communities.

MATERIALS

Yardage is based on 42"-wide fabric. Fat quarters measure approximately 18" x 21". Choose fat quarters with small flowers, checks, dots, etc.

2 yards of white fabric for blocks and appliqué strip (cut lengthwise)

⅝ yard of red print for binding

3 fat quarters of red print for blocks and appliqués

3 fat quarters of aqua print for blocks and appliqués

3 fat quarters of yellow print for blocks and appliqués

3 fat quarters of blue print for blocks and appliqués

4 fat quarters of pink print for blocks and appliqués

4 yards of fabric for backing (pieced horizontally)

2 yards lightweight fusible web for appliqués

62" x 68" piece of batting

Thread in coordinating colors for appliqués

Water-soluble glue stick

1 yard of mini white rickrack (optional)

3½ yards of medium-sized, dark-pink rickrack

CUTTING

All measurements include ¼"-wide seam allowances. Cut all strips across the width of fabric unless otherwise instructed.

The appliqué patterns for pieces A–T are on pages 69–75. For information on preparing and cutting pieces for fusible appliqué, refer to "Fusible Appliqué" on page 8.

From the white fabric, cut *on the lengthwise grain:*

1 strip, 10½" x 64½"

From the remainder of the white fabric, cut:

96 squares, 2⅞" x 2⅞"

192 rectangles, 1½" x 2½"

48 squares, 2½" x 2½"

From *each* of the 16 fat quarters, cut:

6 squares, 2⅞" x 2⅞" (96 total)

6 rectangles, 1½" x 6½" (96 total)

6 rectangles, 1½" x 8½" (96 total)

12 rectangles, 1½" x 2½" (192 total)

For apron 1, choose one blue and one pink fat quarter and cut:

1 A

1 B and 1 reversed

1 C

1 strip, 2" x 20" (no fusible web on this unit)

Continued on page 66

For apron 2, choose two coordinating yellow fat quarters and cut:
1 D
1 E1
1 E2
1 F and 1 reversed
1 G
2 rectangles, 2½" x 3" (no fusible web on these units)

For apron 3, choose two coordinating pink fat quarters and cut:
1 H
1 I
1 J and 1 reversed
1 K
1 L

For apron 4, choose one red fat quarter and cut:
1 M
1 N and 1 reversed
1 O and 1 reversed
1 P
1 rectangle, 2" x 17" (no fusible web on this unit)
2 rectangles, 2" x 8" (no fusible web on this unit)

For apron 5, choose two coordinating aqua fat quarters and cut:
1 Q
2 R
1 S and 1 reversed
1 T

From the red print, cut:
7 strips, 2½" x 42"

MAKING THE BLOCKS

1. Use white fabric and one print to make the pieced center of each block. Referring to "Half-Square-Triangle Units" on page 7, sew a white 2⅞" square and a print 2⅞" square together to make two half-square-triangle units. Press the seam allowances toward the print triangle. Make four half-square-triangle units. Sew a white 1½" x 2½" rectangle to a print 1½" x 2½" rectangle. Make four matching units.

Make 4.   Make 4.

2. Arrange the four half-square-triangle units and the four rectangle units from step 1, and a white 2½" square. Sew the units into horizontal rows. Press the seam allowances as indicated. Sew the rows together. Press the seam allowances away from the center row. The block should measure 6½" x 6½". Make three blocks of each print color for a total of 48 blocks.

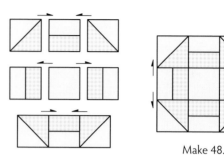

Make 48.

3. Join two different-colored print 1½" x 6½" rectangles to opposite sides of a block from step 2. Join two different-colored print 1½" x 8½" rectangles to the top and bottom. The block should measure 8½" x 8½". Repeat for all 48 blocks.

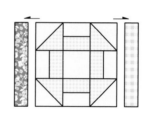 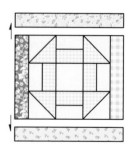

Make 48.

APPLIQUÉING THE APRONS

1. Lay the white 10½" x 64½" appliqué background strip on a large surface. Apron 1 will be at the top, followed by aprons 2, 3, 4, and 5.
2. **For apron 1,** fold the pink 2" x 20" strip in half with right sides together, matching raw edges. Stitch ¼" from each end. Turn the ruffle

right side out and sew a gathering stitch a scant ¼" from the raw edge.

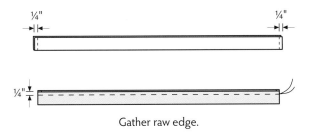

Gather raw edge.

3. Place appliqué pieces A, B, and C on the background, using a small dot of glue to hold them in place. Pin or glue the raw edges of the gathered ruffle under unit A and then fuse and stitch all pieces in place.

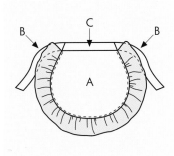

4. **For apron 2,** fold each of the two yellow 2½" x 3" rectangles in half with right sides together and 2½" sides aligned. Stitch across the top and bottom of the folded rectangles. Leave open the side opposite the fold. Turn the pockets right side out and press. Add decorative stitching to pockets and bodice of D if desired, referring to "Decorative Stitching" on page 9.

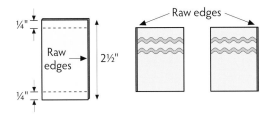

5. Place appliqué pieces D, E1, E2, F, and G on the white background, using a small dot of glue to hold them in place. Place the pockets wrong side up with the raw edge tucked under the apron sides (E1 and E2). Carefully fuse the pieces in place, catching the raw edges of the pocket under the apron E pieces. Stitch around all pieces, except the pockets. You will catch the raw edges of the pockets under apron E pieces when stitching. After stitching, fold the pockets back onto the apron sides and stitch the pieces in place, leaving the pockets open at the top.

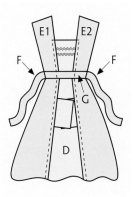

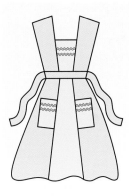

6. **For apron 3,** arrange the H, I, J, K, and L appliqué pieces on the center of the white strip. Fuse and stitch the appliqués in place.

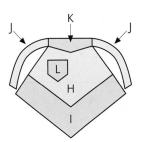

7. **For apron 4,** hem the long edges of the 2" x 17" strip and the two 2" x 8" strips by using a rolled hem foot or turning under ¼" and stitching. Turn each short end of the strips under ¼" and topstitch. Trim the longer strip to 1" wide; it should measure 1" x 16½". Trim the two shorter strips to ⅞" wide; they should measure ⅞" x 7½". Stitch a gathering thread along the raw edge of each strip and gather gently to create a ruffle.

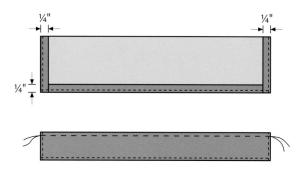

8. Glue or pin baste each ruffle in place, pulling gathers as needed so they fit. Tuck the ⅞" x 7½" pieces under the outer edge of bodice pieces (N) and under the waistband (P). Tuck apron ties (O) under the waistband (P). Tuck the 1" x 16½" ruffle under the bottom edge of the apron (M). Fuse and stitch all pieces in place. Add decorative stitching or mini white rick-rack as desired.

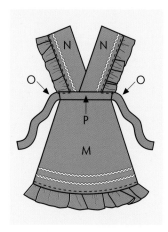

9. **For apron 5,** sew two pockets (R) with right sides together, using a scant ¼"-wide seam allowance and leaving an opening between the marked dots. Clip the corners, turn right side out and press.

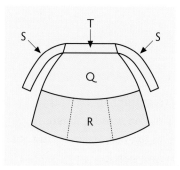

Leave open.

10. Lay the Q, S, and T appliqué pieces on the white background. Fuse the pieces in place. Pin or glue baste the pocket unit over the bottom of the apron. Stitch the pieces in place, including around the left, right, and bottom edges of the pocket; the stitching will secure the opening where the pocket was turned. Stitch two straight lines as indicated on the pattern to make three separate pockets.

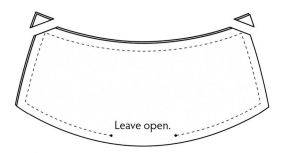

ASSEMBLING THE QUILT TOP

1. Arrange the blocks, including the apron panel, on a large surface to achieve good color balance. Rotate the blocks in each row so the longest strips of the blocks alternate horizontally and vertically from block to block and row to row.

2. Sew the eight blocks on the left side of the apron panel into a vertical row. Press the seam allowances in one direction. Sew the vertical row to the left side of the apron panel. Press the seam allowances toward the blocks. Sew the remaining eight rows of five blocks together. Press the seam allowances in opposite directions from row to row. Sew the rows together. Press the seam allowances in one

direction. Sew the eight rows to the right side of the apron strip. Press the seam allowances toward the blocks.

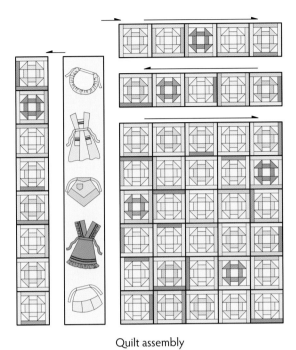

Quilt assembly

FINISHING THE QUILT

Refer to "Finishing" on page 9 as needed.

1. Layer the quilt top, batting, and backing (pieced horizontally); baste. Quilt as desired. I used an overall, meandering, small floral design and stitched around each apron to give definition.
2. Sew medium-sized, dark-pink rickrack on top of the seams that join the apron panel to the pieced blocks.
3. Using the red 2½"-wide strips, sew the binding to the quilt.

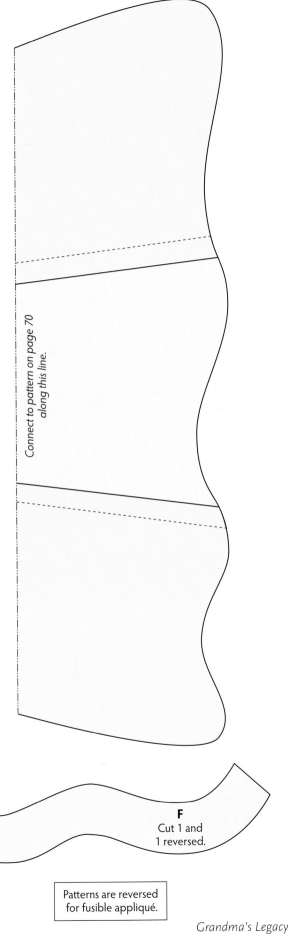

Connect to pattern on page 70 along this line.

F
Cut 1 and
1 reversed.

Patterns are reversed for fusible appliqué.

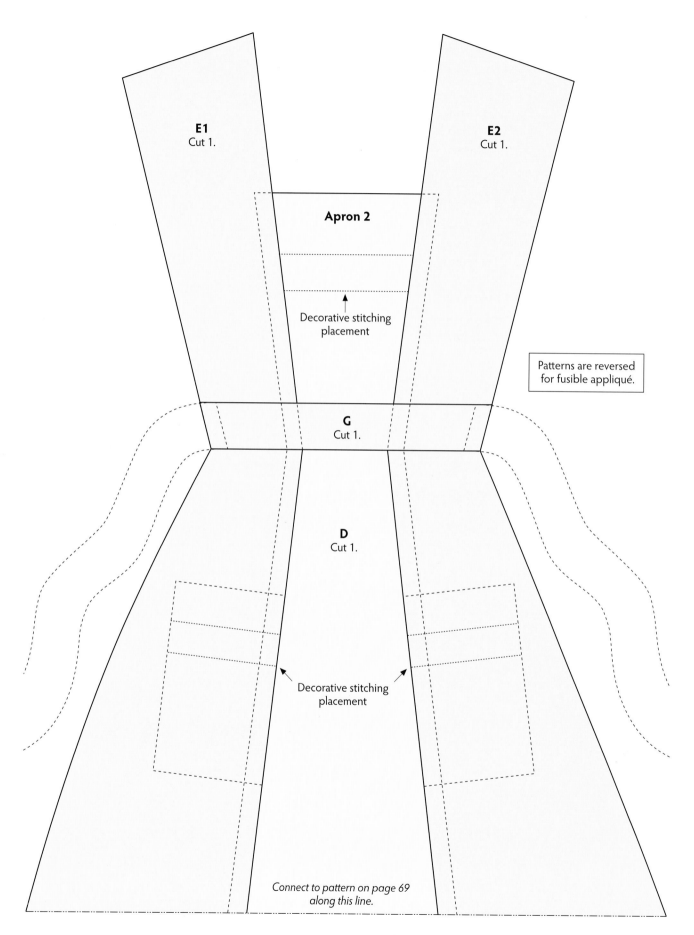

E1
Cut 1.

E2
Cut 1.

Apron 2

Decorative stitching placement

Patterns are reversed for fusible appliqué.

G
Cut 1.

D
Cut 1.

Decorative stitching placement

Connect to pattern on page 69 along this line.

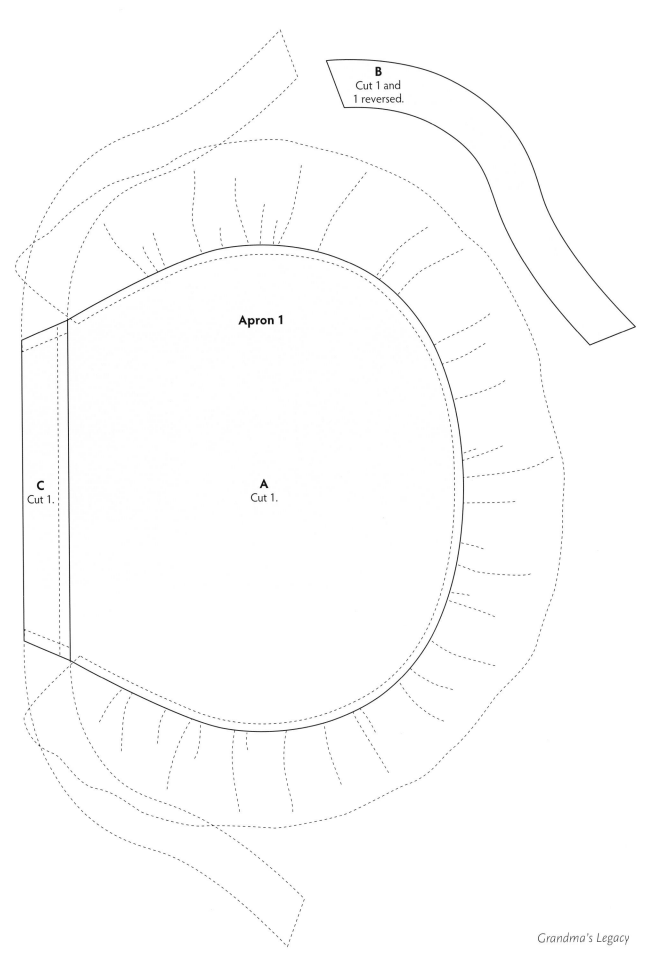

B
Cut 1 and
1 reversed.

Apron 1

C
Cut 1.

A
Cut 1.

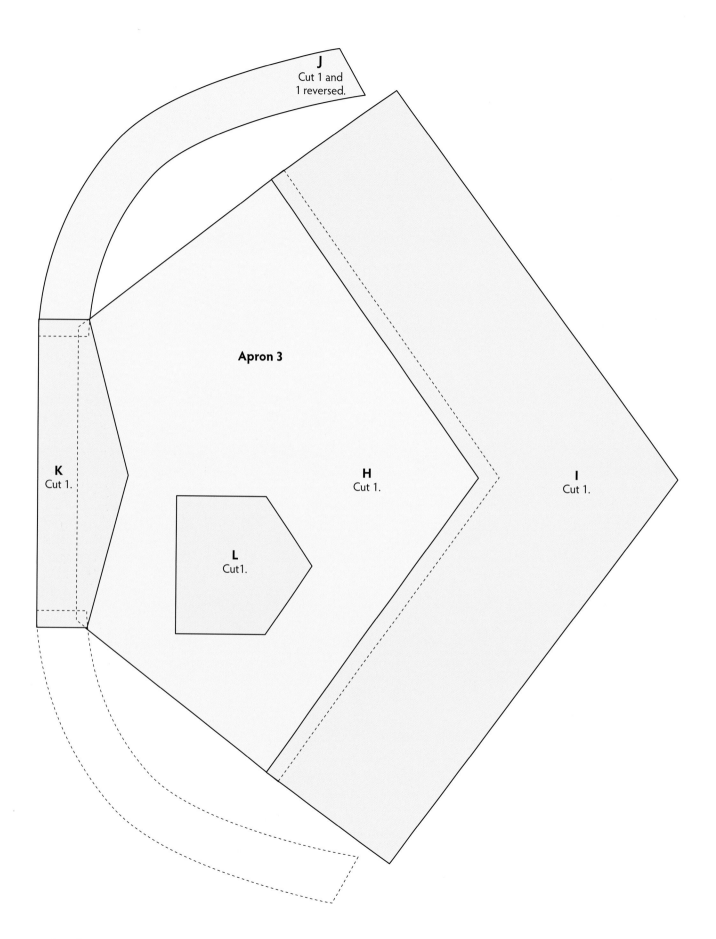

J
Cut 1 and
1 reversed.

Apron 3

K
Cut 1.

H
Cut 1.

I
Cut 1.

L
Cut1.

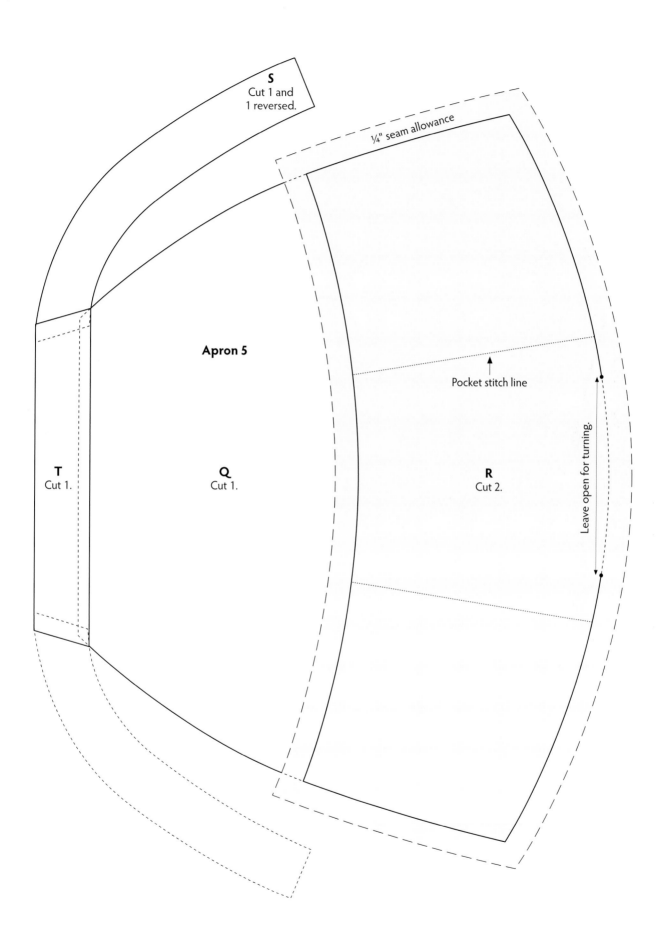

S
Cut 1 and
1 reversed.

¼" seam allowance

Apron 5

Pocket stitch line

Leave open for turning.

T
Cut 1.

Q
Cut 1.

R
Cut 2.

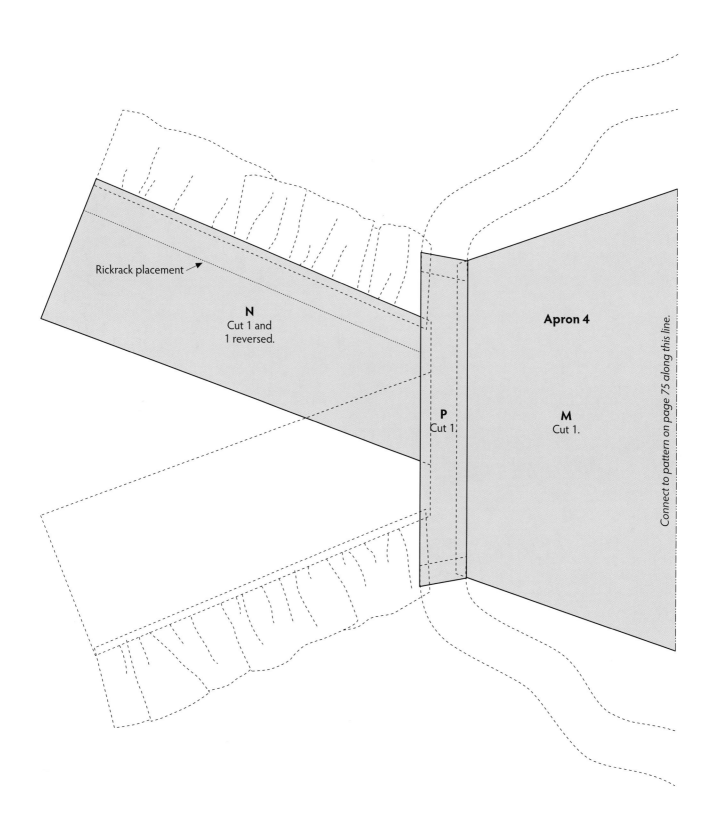

Rickrack placement

N
Cut 1 and
1 reversed.

Apron 4

P
Cut 1.

M
Cut 1.

Connect to pattern on page 75 along this line.

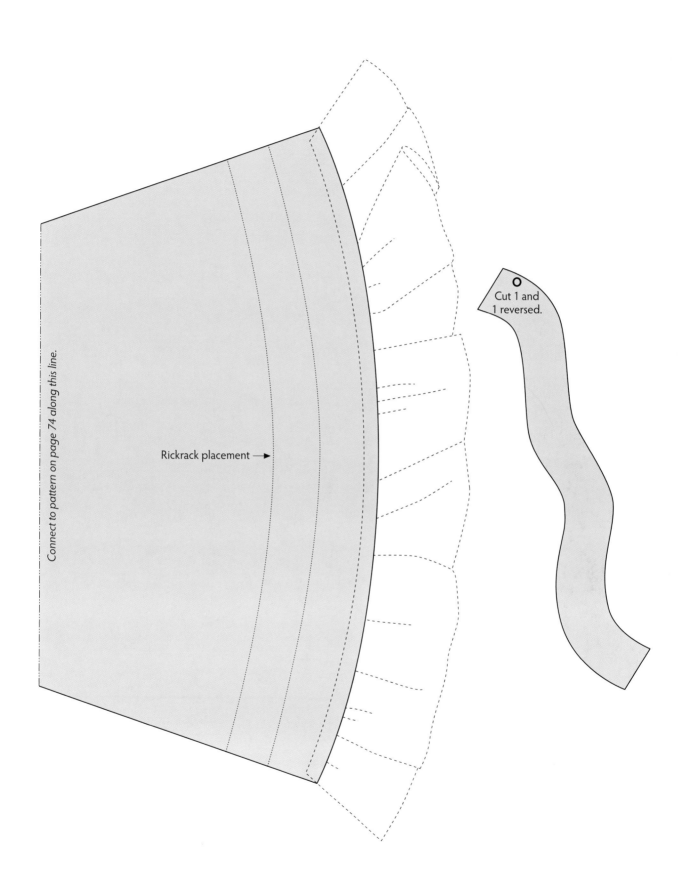

Connect to pattern on page 74 along this line.

Rickrack placement →

Cut 1 and
1 reversed.

Designed, pieced, and quilted by Geralyn Powers

FINISHED QUILT: 56½" x 64½" ▪ FINISHED BLOCK: 8" x 8"

Daisies All Around

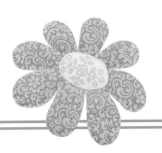

Renowned poet Ralph Waldo Emerson once said, "Earth laughs in flowers." This quilt is laughing in daisies and it's a lovely sound. Paired with a traditional block made from half-square-triangle units, the simple appliquéd flowers make a charming statement. This is a delightful design that would make a great bed covering, throw, or thoughtful gift.

MATERIALS

Yardage is based on 42"-wide fabric. Fat quarters measure approximately 18" x 21".

1½ yards of cream marbled print (borders are cut on the lengthwise grain)
¾ yard *each* of two different aqua prints for blocks and flowers
10 fat quarters of assorted cream and aqua prints for blocks and flower centers
2 yards of lightweight fusible web for appliqués
4 yards of fabric for backing
⅝ yard of aqua print for binding
60" x 72" piece of batting
Threads in coordinating colors for appliqués

CUTTING

All measurements include ¼"-wide seam allowances. Cut all strips across the width of fabric unless otherwise instructed.

The appliqué patterns for pieces A and B are on page 79. For information on preparing and cutting pieces for fusible appliqué, refer to "Fusible Appliqué" on page 8.

From the assorted cream and aqua print fat quarters, cut:
116 squares, 4⅞" x 4⅞"

From *each* of the two aqua prints for blocks and flowers, cut:
10 squares, 4⅞" x 4⅞" (20 total)

From the cream marbled print, cut *on the lengthwise grain:*
2 strips, 8½" x 48½"
2 strips, 8½" x 40½"

From the aqua print for binding, cut:
7 strips, 2½" x 42"

From *each* of the two aqua prints for flowers, cut:
9 A (18 total)

From the assorted fat quarters, cut:
18 B

MAKING THE BLOCKS

1. Using two contrasting 4⅞" squares and referring to "Half-Square-Triangle Units" on page 7, make two half-square-triangle units. Press the seam allowances toward the darker triangle. The units should measure 4½" x 4½". Repeat to make 136 units.

Make 136.

2. Join four units from step 1. Press the seam allowances as indicated. The block should measure 8½" x 8½". Make 20 blocks.

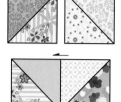 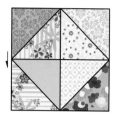

Make 20.

ASSEMBLING THE QUILT TOP

1. Arrange the blocks in five rows of four blocks each. Sew the blocks together in rows. Press the seam allowances in opposite directions from row to row. Sew the rows together. Press the seam allowances in one direction.

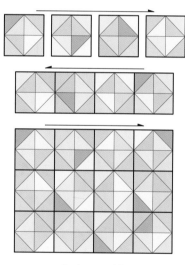

Quilt assembly

2. Arrange four flowers with centers, alternating the two aqua colors, onto a cream 8½" x 40½" strip. Fuse and stitch the appliqués in place. Make two appliquéd strips. Arrange five flowers with centers, also alternating the two aqua

colors, onto a cream 8½" x 48½" strip. Fuse and stitch the appliqués in place. Make two appliquéd strips.

Make 2.

Make 2.

3. Join 12 half-square-triangle units to make a top/bottom border. Press the seam allowances in one direction. Make two top/bottom borders. Join 16 half-square-triangle units to make a side border. Press the seam allowances in one direction. Make two side borders.

Top/bottom border.
Make 2.

Side border.
Make 2.

4. Sew the 8½" x 40½" flower borders to opposite sides of the quilt. Press the seam allowances toward the flower borders. Sew the 8½" x 48½" flower borders to the top and bottom of the quilt. Press the seam allowances toward the flower borders. Sew the 12-unit pieced borders to the top and bottom of the quilt. Press the seam allowances toward the flower borders. Sew the 16-unit pieced borders to opposite sides of the quilt. Press the seam allowances toward the flower borders.

Border assembly

FINISHING THE QUILT

Refer to "Finishing" on page 9 as needed.

1. Layer the quilt top, batting, and backing (pieced horizontally); baste. Quilt as desired. I used an overall, small floral design on the blocks and a medium-size stipple on the appliqué background.

2. Using the aqua 2½"-wide strips, sew the binding to the quilt.

Patterns are reversed for fusible appliqué.

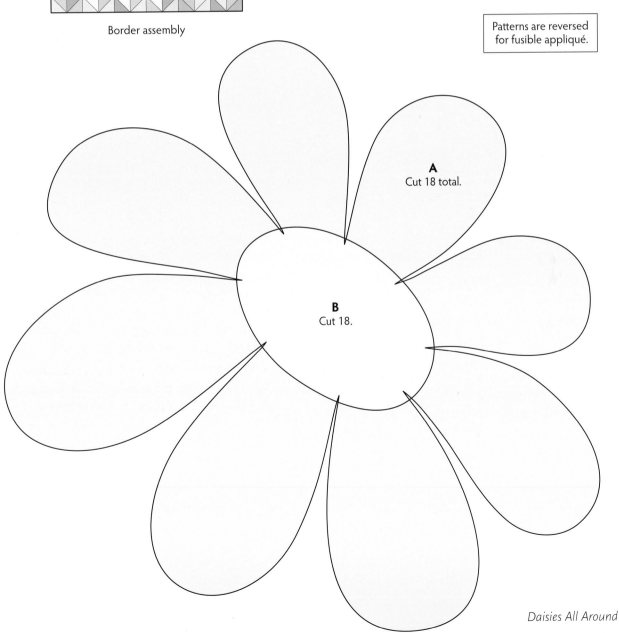

A
Cut 18 total.

B
Cut 18.

Resources

The raisin buttons can
be purchased at
Valley Fabric Shop
102 Mt. Meadow Street
Lyman, WY 82937
307-786-2653
Email: valleyfab@union-tel.com

Acknowledgments

It is impossible for me to sew
anything and not give thanks
to Jean Payne, a mentor, friend,
wonderful 4-H leader, and
teacher, whose lessons and
example have been a tremen-
dous influence for good and
learning in my life.

I am grateful to my parents
for recognizing my love for creativity at an early age and for
encouraging and supporting it
in every way.

Lastly, I am appreciative
of Charla Youngberg, Bobbi
Clark, and all the lovely ladies
at Valley Fabric Shop for allowing me to learn while I have
tried to teach quilting skills. It
has been a grand journey, and
I hope it continues for many
years. Charla and Bobbi have
given me many opportunities
for experience, success, and
friendship. I am thankful for
their association, the laughs,
the "does this work?" discus-
sions, and all the joys that go
with great quilting friends.

About the Author

Creativity has been a part of my life for as long as I can remember. I grew up around strong, accomplished women and watched them express their creativity while caring for homes and families. It is an amazing lesson to learn from others that in the midst of the many demands of life, one can choose to be expressive in functional tasks. Both of my grandmothers excelled at sewing and quilting arts and helped me develop those skills. I was fortunate to participate in 4-H and, with the help of great leaders, I learned one can have a grand time while reaching for technical and artistic excellence. I graduated from college with a BS in Clothing and Textiles and then promptly moved with my husband to a small Wyoming community that provided few merchandising opportunities. Luckily, our little town has a fabulous quilt shop that is my "home away from home."

I have taken the opportunity of designing quilt patterns and teaching lots of classes. Quilters are some of the loveliest people, and I have learned so much in teaching and associating with such talented ladies. Nothing fosters creativity more than others who share its value.

My greatest joy comes from my family. I am blessed with a very supportive husband, a son, a daughter, a beautiful daughter-in-law, and three wonderful grandchildren.